Coyle's New Convert
Bible
Commentary

M R Coyle

James C. Winston
Publishing Company, Inc.

Trade Division of Winston-Derek Publishers Group, Inc.

PUBLISHED BY JAMES C. WINSTON PUBLISHING COMPANY, INC.
Nashville, Tennessee 37205

Library of Congress Catalog Card No: 93-60352
ISBN: 1-55523-617-0

Printed in the United States of America

To Phyllis Estep

CONTENTS

STUDY TO SHOW THYSELF APPROVED UNTO GOD,
A WORKMAN THAT NEEDETH NOT TO BE ASHAMED,
RIGHTLY DIVIDING THE WORD OF TRUTH.

II TIMOTHY 2:15

INTRODUCTION

The Holy Bible is the most fascinating book every written; it is the cornerstone of Western Civilization, a book more widely quoted than any other; it has survived almost 3,000 years and outlived those nations and empires which attempted to destroy it. We all know of it, but few of us really *know* it: the living word of God, God breathed (II Tim. 3:16), more powerful than a two-edged sword, the surest way to find God's will for us both as individuals and nations, yet it remains a mystery. It was not intended to be so. This book is a summary or map to help the reader begin a journey into God's word. Once you have begun, the best commentary on the Bible is the Bible, because it is the "living word." Through its pages God speaks directly to your heart.

The Bible is divided into two parts: The Old Testament and The New Testament. The Old Testament refers to the period of history before the incarnation (birth of Christ). It contains the account of creation (Genesis); the fall of man, and God's plan for his restoration; the history of the Jewish people together with prophetic books and books of Hebrew poetry and praise. The New Testament deals with the life, death, and resurrection of Our Lord, the growth of the early church, letters of instruction in the faith, and the Revelation of St. John the Divine. The Catholic Bible contains also some apocryphal books (inter-testament) not accepted as canonical by the reformed church.

OVERVIEW

In 2090 B.C. the Jewish nation began with the call of Abraham (Gen. 12). Abraham's genealogy is given in Genesis 11; he is descended from Noah's son, Shem, and there are nine generations from Shem to Abraham.

Abraham's call was to walk before God and be blameless (Gen. 17:1). God's promise to Abraham was:

> I will make you into a great nation and I will bless you; I will make your name great and you will be a blessing. I will bless those who bless you and whoever curses you I will curse and all the peoples on earth will be blessed through you.
> Gen. 12:2–3

Abraham left Haran in Upper Mesopotamia and was led by the Spirit to Canaan. There God "gave" Abraham the land of Canaan and instituted circumcision as a sign of the covenant relationship between them. Abraham had eight sons: Ishmael, Isaac, Zimran, Jokshan, Medan, Midian, Ishbak, and Shuah. It is through his second, Isaac, that the covenant descended.

Isaac, whose name means laughter, was a miracle baby born when Abraham's first wife Sarah was over ninety. The ultimate test of Abraham's faith came when Isaac was grown—Abraham was ordered to sacrifice his son to God. As Abraham prepared to obey (without questioning), God prevented the sacrifice from taking place. He was satisfied with Abraham's total commitment. This shows both the steadfastness of Abraham's faith and conveys the degree of Isaac's submission to the will of God. It also shows a distinctive feature of the Jewish faith—the practice of sacrificing children to local deities to obtain favor was widespread in Canaan. The Jewish religion specifically forbids this; in fact anyone doing so is to be stoned to death (Lev. 18:21, 20:2).

The book of Genesis details Abraham's family history. Abraham's son Isaac had two sons, Jacob and Esau. Jacob—also known as Israel—had twelve sons, the patriarchs from whom the twelve tribes of Israel are descended. Jacob's favorite son was Joseph (1904–1804 B.C.). Joseph had prophetic dreams. Spurred on by jealousy and hatred, his brothers sold Joseph into slavery (1897 B.C.); despite this Joseph remained true to God, even when falsely accused of molesting his owner's wife and imprisoned. In prison Joseph interpreted the dreams of Pharaoh's chief butler and baker. His interpretations proved correct. When two years later Pharaoh was troubled with prophetic dreams the butler remembered Joseph. Joseph was sent for and was able to prophesy that Egypt would have seven years of abundance and plentiful harvests followed by seven years of severe famine. Joseph suggested that Pharaoh stockpile a tax of 20% of the harvest during the good years so that reserves would be on hand for the years of famine. Pharaoh (possibly Senusert II, 1894–1878 B.C.) appointed Joseph Vizier. During the reign of his successor Senusert III, Pharaoh broke the power of the nobility selling them back this corn in exchange for their land and freedom.

Canaan also suffered from the famine, and Jacob sent Joseph's brothers to Egypt to buy corn. On their first trip Joseph did not make himself known but insisted that if they returned, Benjamin must be brought with them. (Jacob had four wives; only Joseph and Benjamin were from his favorite wife Rachel.) On the second trip Joseph laid a trap for his brothers. He made it appear as though Benjamin had stolen his divination cup. Joseph wanted to test his half-brothers and see if they still hated the favored sons of Rachel and would abandon Benjamin. However, his brothers had learned their lesson; Judah volunteered to be a slave in Benjamin's place to make reparation for the theft. Moved, Joseph revealed his true identity and sent an invitation to his father to join him. In 1875 B.C. Jacob went to live in Egypt (fulfilling the word given to Abraham in Genesis 15:13).

After the expulsion of the Semitic Hykos kings c1550 B.C., the Pharaohs of the eighteenth dynasty began a series of military campaigns in Palestine and Syria. Egypt conquered territory from the river Euphrates to the fourth cataract of the Nile. The oppression of subject peoples including the Israelites began. Enslaved, the Hurrians, Canaanites, Israelites and Amorites undertook the building of Pharaoh's cities and tombs. The Lord had compassion on Israel and raised up Moses as deliverer. Moses is a common Egyptian name, Ms meaning to be born. Descended from the tribe of Levi, reared at the Egyptian court, Moses yearned to free his people. Seeing an Egyptian overseer whipping a Hebrew, he killed the Egyptian and became a fugitive. He fled to Midian where he spent forty years in the desert, learning patience and humility. Being stripped of all his princely pride, Moses was finally ready to be used as God's instrument.

Moses was understandably reluctant to return to Egypt, but at the Lords command he went. Together with Aaron he pleaded with Pharaoh to release the Israelites. When Pharaoh refused, YHWH afflicted Egypt with ten plagues, the last one—the death of the firstborn—being the one that finally broke Pharaoh's spirit.

The achievement of Moses in leading the Israelites to the promised land cannot be overestimated. He led approximately one million people through the desert! The people he led were "stiffnecked and rebellious." Frightened to fight, frightened to move, they grumbled, frequently challenged his authority and even built idols while Moses was on Mt. Sinai receiving the Ten Commandments. Upon reaching the promised land, Moses sent twelve spies out to investigate the land. The spies returned bringing back a report that the land was indeed "flowing with milk and honey," but the inhabitants lived in walled cities and had impressive armies! The gaggle of slaves was no match for well trained and well armed armies. The people became discouraged and once more grumbled against Moses. The Lord then told them to turn back into the desert; none of those who had grumbled against him would enter the promised land. Two of the spies, Joshua and Caleb, were convinced that with YHWH they would conquer, and they were spared from YHWH's curse. Joshua 1 describes the call upon Joshua's life. Joshua led the people across the Jordan, which miraculously dried up when the feet of the priests carrying the ark touched the water. Joshua's appointment as leader was confirmed with a second miraculous sign: the collapse of the walls of Jerico after his men circled it and raised a shout of triumph. This happened around 1405 B.C., and archeological evidence exists showing that in approximately 1400 B.C. the walls of Jerico fell. Joshua captured south Canaan in a series of swift moving battles. Joshua's army was no match for the Canaanites in a fair fight, so Joshua relied heavily on the elements of surprise and deception. The kings of North Canaan, headed by Jabin, King of Hazor, united to withstand the Israelite invasion and were equally unsuccessful. Their horses were hamstrung, their chariots were burned and they were resoundingly defeated at Merom. Joshua portioned the land and dismissed the eastern tribes exhorting them to "Love the Lord your God, to walk in all his ways, to obey his commands, to hold fast to him and to serve him with all your heart and soul," (Josh. 22:25). Joshua renewed the covenant at Shechem and died.

Israel had served YHWH and enjoyed the fruits of obedience and allegiance to YHWH, however succeeding generations fell into worshipping the various Canaanite deities, the most popular being various Baals and Ashtaroth. These gods personified natural forces and their rituals included illicit sex and child sacrificeboth of which were abominations in the sight of YHWH.

The book of Judges describes the struggle between a backsliding Israel and surrounding pagan nations. Israel would worship false gods; YHWH would allow them to be conquered. They would then repent and the Lord would raise up a "judge" or deliverer. The most famous of the judges was Samson, whose glamorized life story has been popularized by Hollywood. Samson waged a one-man war against the Philistines who were oppressing/ruling over Israel. The Philistines were great warriors, even venturing to attack Egypt c1200 b.c. apparently in alliance with the Hebrew tribe of Dan. Other famous judges include Deborah the only woman judge—who with general Barak prevented the Canaanites from driving a wedge through central Canaan and cutting off the northern tribes, and Gideon who broke the Midianite yoke, though he himself built an ephod. The time of the judges was a time when there was no central authority in Israel and men did as they saw fit. The tribe of Benjamin lapsed into sexual deviancy and was nearly destroyed (Judges 19–21) and the tribe of Dan migrated north. The last great judge of Israel was the prophet Samuel. Samuel was promised to God before birth by his mother Hannah and given to the priest Eli at the temple. Like Samson he lived during the time of Philistine oppression. During this period the tribes realized their need for unification. Despite Samuel and YHWH leading them to victory at Mizpah in 1047 b.c., the leaders demanded a king in order to be like all other nations (I Sam. 8). Saul, son of Kish, a Benjamite was chosen as the Lord's anointed. He was an imposing figure, "a man without equal among the

Israelites, a head taller than any of the others." He was appointed king c1043 B.C. and quickly proved himself, defeating the Ammonites at Jabesh Gilead. Following this victory, Saul was reannointed at Gilgal. However, the Israelites main enemy were the Philistines. Israel was so completely subjugated to the Philistines that the Israelites had no weapons; the Philistines forbade it (I Sam. 13:19). The Philistines determined to destroy the kingdom before it became established, so after Jonathan captured Giba they assembled an army of 3,000 chariots and 6,000 horses. Saul retreated to Gilgal and found his army deserting. Impatiently he decided not to wait for the arrival of Samuel and sacrificed the burnt offering. Because Saul acted inappropriately Samuel prophesied the kingdom would be given to another, a king who would obey YHWH. After Jonathan's surprise attack on the Philistine outpost at Michmash, where he wiped out a Philistine garrison, the Lord sent a panic among the Philistines, and Hebrew mercenaries in the Philistine army rejoined Saul and Jonathan. A great Hebrew victory ensued with a wholesale slaughter of the Philistines. The Philistines could not allow Saul to continue, Israel was becoming too strong. They assembled so vast an army that it was impossible for Saul to win; assembling at Aphek they launched an attack and destroyed Saul's army at Mt. Gilboa. Saul and his dynasty were destroyed 1011 B.C.

The second King of Israel, David (ruled 1001–961 B.C.) was a very different man. Described as a man after YHWH's own heart, David was anointed by Samuel after Saul usurped the priestly function and sacrificed without Samuel. Though anointed he did not try to take the kingdom from his master, instead he entered Saul's service and won renown as a commander. "Saul has slain his thousands and David his tens of thousands" sang the crowds. David was totally devoted to YHWH. He is famous for slaying the giant Goliath who championed the Philistine armies. Facing the armored giant, armed only with slingshots, the youngster declared:

> You come against me with sword and spear and javelin, but I come against you in the name of the Lord Almighty, the God of the armies of Israel, whom you have defied. This day the Lord will hand you over to me. . . .

During David's reign, Israel reached the zenith of her power. It is not accidental that this was also the peak of Israel's spiritual power. During David's reign the boundaries of worship were stretched to their widest extent. David wrote many of the Psalms, continually exhorting us to "Sing joyfully to the Lord you righteous, it is fitting for the upright to praise him, Praise him with the harp, make music to him on the ten-stringed lyre. Sing to him a new song, play skillfully and shout for joy, (Ps. 33).

> Praise him with the sounding of the trumpet
> Praise him with the harp and lyre,
> Praise him with tambourine and dancing,
> Praise him with the strings and flute,
> Praise him with the clash of cymbals,
> Praise him with resounding cymbals.
>
> Ps. 150

David began his empire, establishing his capital at Jerusalem. Nominally within the territory allotted to Benjamin—but never fully captured—no one tribe would be exalted by this choice. Jerusalem was also close to the border with Judah, David's own tribe. David conquered Jerusalem in 1005 B.C. but spared most of its inhabitants. The ark was transferred to Jerusalem and David made preparations for the building of a magnificent temple. David decisively defeated the Philistines and conquered the Jezreel valley. Edom and Moab were brought under Israelite domination. David survived attempted coups by members of his own family twice and had Solomon proclaimed King while he was still alive. Solomon, famed for his wisdom and wealth, is a romantic figure. Born of David's favorite wife Bathsheba he was no warrior king, but a diplomat and administrator. He fully exploited Israel's strategic position between Mesopotamia and Egypt. He is reputed to have written Proverbs, Ecclesiastes, and the Song of Songs. Jewish legend has it that he had an affair with the Queen of Sheba. God appeared to Solomon twice at the beginning of his reign; both times Solomon asked for wisdom to govern Israel. Despite this promising start Solomon began to worship false gods. He had many wives including a daughter of Pharaoh, and these wives led him into worshipping their gods. Due to this infidelity Israel was weakened and by the end of his reign the vast empire built up by David was ready to crumble. After Solomon's death he was succeeded by his son Rehoboam (931–913 B.C.). Rehoboam found himself facing a discontent nation. On his accession, the northern tribes under Jeroboam asked the young king to relax the harsh taxation imposed by Solomon. Rehoboam refused and rebellion ensued. He was forced to flee to Jerusalem, while Jeroboam fortified Shechem and assumed kingship of Israel.

This splitting of the kingdom lead to the decline and enslaving of both kingdoms. In the following years the Kings of Israel, the northern kingdom, promoted idol worship in an attempt to keep the kingdom from reverting into the hands of the Kings of Judah. Jeroboam built Golden Calves at Bethel and Dan to prevent the Israelites from worshipping at Jerusalem. Jeroboam's dynasty did not last long; his son Nabad was murdered by Baasa, whose dynasty also ended in bloodshed. Omri (885–874 B.C.) moved the capital to Samaria. His son Ahab (874–853 B.C.) married the infamous Jezebel from Tyre in Phoenicia. This alliance brought a great deal of wealth to Israel, but it also brought Baal worship. "Ahab did more to provoke the Lord, the God of Israel, to anger than did all the kings of Israel before him," (I Kings 17:33).

It was during the reign of Ahab that the great prophet Elijah ministered. Elijah pronounced God's judgement, in the form of a drought on Israel. After three and a half years of drought, the Lord told Elijah to present himself to Ahab and the Lord would send rain. Elijah met Obadiah, Ahab's servant, and summoned the king. Ahab agreed to summon the prophets of Baal to Mount Carmel. There Elijah challenged Israel, "How long will you waver between two opinions? If the Lord is God, follow him, but if Baal is God, follow him," (I Kings 18:21). Each side built an altar and called on the name of their God. From morning to noon the priests called on Baal with no response. Elijah called, once, and the fire fell and burned up the sacrifice. Elijah then slaughtered the prophets of Baal and ended the drought. Despite Ahab's idolatry the Lord gave him victory over the Armenians. Later he died in battle at Ramoth Gilead after ignoring prophetic warning. His dynasty was wiped out by Jehu (841–814 B.C.). It was during the reign of Jehu that Israel began to feel the might of the Assyrians.

Up until the middle of the eighth century B.C. the Assyrians wanted plunder, but Tiger Pileser III (745–727 B.C.) wanted territorial expansion. Israel under Pekah decided to resist and tried to force Ahaz of Judah to join him. Ahaz appealed to Assyria for help. The Assyrians conquered Galilee and Gilead. Pekah was murdered and succeeded by his son Hoshea. Hoshea served Assyria until 727 B.C. when Shalmaneser V became king, then he decided to chance rebellion. He began negotiating with Egypt for help; it never came. The Assyrian king moved quickly and crushed the rebellion, Samaria surrendering in 722 B.C. On Shalmaneser V's death Samaria once more rebelled and in 720 Sargon II defeated the rebels and made Samaria capital of a new Assyrian province called Samarina. The northern kingdom had been effectively annihilated. This fulfilled the prophecies of among others Amos & Hosea who warned the Israelite kings to repent while their was time.

The kingdom of Judah fared somewhat better. While the dynasties of Israel were short-lived and ended in bloodshed, the royal house of Judah remained intact. In fact Jesus' human lineage is traceable back to King David.

After the kingdom split in two in 931 B.C. Rehoboam fled back to Jerusalem and mustered an army of 18,000 men, but the Lord warned him not to fight Israel. Rehoboam obeyed, but fortified the border towns. Jeroboam's patron, the Egyptian pharaoh Shishak attacked Jerusalem in 926 B.C. and carried off most of the treasures King Solomon had installed there. Rehoboam's son Abijah succeeded in defeating Jeroboam in battle. Unlike his father, Abijah was devoted to YHWH, he addressed the opposing army of Israel prior to the battle thus: "God is with us. He is our leader. His priests with their trumpets will sound the battle cry against you. Men of Israel do not fight against the Lord, the God of your fathers, for you will not succeed." And Judah did indeed prove victorious. Both Abijah's son (Asa) and grandson (Jehoshaphat) were extremely dedicated to God and they both extended Judah's power. In fact the surrounding kingdoms paid tribute to Judah (I Chron. 17:10). Unfortunately, Jehoshaphat chose to make a marriage alliance with Ahab the idolatrous king of Israel. He joined Ahab at the disastrous battle of Ramoth-Gilead where Israel and Judah were defeated by the Armenians and Ahab was killed. Jehoshaphat returned to Jerusalem where he was rebuked by the prophet Jehu for helping the wicked. He soon found himself facing a powerful alliance of enemy kings; Moab, Ammon, and Menites attacked him. Hopelessly outnumbered Jehoshaphat ordered the army to praise God, and as they did so the Lord sent ambushes against their enemies.

The fear of God came upon all the kingdoms of the countries when they heard how the Lord had fought against the enemies of Israel. And the Kingdom of Jehoshophat was at peace for the Lord had given him rest on every side.

II Chron. 20:29–30

Due to the alliance with the house of Ahab, Jehoshaphat's son was Ahab's grandson and "did evil in the eyes of the Lord." Judah's dominance began to fade. The Philistines and Arabs invaded Judah. Jehoram's son Ahaziah was also wicked. He was closely allied to Jerom of Israel and when Jehu's rebellion broke out he perished with his kinsman. Athaliah—Ahaziah's mother and Omri's granddaughter—seized the Judean throne. She murdered all of the royal princes, except for Joash who was hidden by his sister and so escaped. Athaliah reigned for six years. At the end of that time the priest, Jehoiada, arranged a coup and put the young king back on the throne. Joash, reared by the priests, began his reign well, repairing the temple, but after the death of Jehoiada he too turned to idol worship and was responsible for the death of Zedekiah (the son of Jehoiada). Shortly after Zedekiah's murder, Judah was overrun by the Armenians and the king was himself assassinated. His son's reign was equally disastrous and idolatrous. The next king, Uzziah, was a faithful king and during his reign many prophets were active. He extended the Judean sphere of influence over the Philistines and Ammonites and his fame reached Egypt. During his reign, and his son's, Judah enjoyed a period of peace and power. However, the Assyrian empire had already extended its influence as far as Damascus. Pekah, King of Israel (752–732 B.C.), headed an alliance against the Assyrians, but Ahaz of Judah (735–715 B.C.) wanted an alliance with Assyria and bribed Tiger-Pilsner with the temple gold! Impressed with the Assyrians' might, Ahaz decided to worship their gods.

Ahaz's son, Hezekiah, was one of the greatest kings of Judah, and was responsible for leading the next great rebellion, in coalition with the Phoenicians and Philistines, against Assyria in 705 B.C.

Hezekiah was willing to be guided by the prophet Isaiah. In fact in 701 B.C. when the Assyrians, after capturing the fortress of Lacish, demanded the surrender of Jerusalem, Hezekiah turned to Isaiah for advice and help. The Bible records that the Angel of the Lord annihilated all the fighting men of Assyria—185,000 in one night and Sennacherib withdrew. Jerusalem was saved, but Judah was devastated and Hezekiah ruled over a reduced land and had to put up with Assyrian domination. His son Manasseh was briefly taken captive by the Assyrians.

The Assyrians were the terror of the near east. Their army is vividly described in Joel. Their power reached its zenith under Esarhaddon and Assurbanipal. The destruction was foretold by the prophet Nahum, but nevertheless it shook the ancient world. During the reign of Hezekiah's great grandson Josiah (640–609 B.C.) the Babylonian empire rose to prominence. In 626 B.C. Nabopolassar seized the Babylonian throne and by 615 Babylon was a threat to Assyria. When the Medes attacked the Assyrians in 614 B.C. the Babylonians formed an alliance with them and in 612 the Assyrian capital of Nineveh fell to the combined Babylonian and Median armies. The Assyrians regrouped at Haran and appealed to Egypt for help. The fear which Babylon generated is measured by the fact that Pharaoh Neco decided to help. Josiah of Judah would not allow the Egyptian army to pass through unchallenged and forced them to meet him in battle at Meggido. Though Josiah was defeated and died, this delay meant that the Egyptians arrived too late to fight at Haran. In 609 B.C. Assurballit, the last Assyrian king, and the Egyptians attempted to retake Haran; they failed and Assurballit disappeared.

The fall of the Assyrian empire left a power vacuum which both Egypt and Babylon strove to fill. Josiah's defeat and death in

609 B.C. meant that Judah was under Egyptian control. However when Babylon defeated the remnants of the Assyrians and the Egyptians at Carchemish in 605 B.C. control shifted. In Judah there were both Egyptian and Babylonians factions. In 601 B.C., despite the prophesies and warnings of Jeremiah, Jehoiakim allied himself with Egypt. This lead to Nebuchadnezzar's attack on Jerusalem in 597 B.C. King Jehoiakim was taken prisoner and the temple was plundered. His son and successor, Jehoiachin, was also imprisoned by Nebuchadnezzar. Zedekiah, the last Judean king ruled from 597–587 B.C. Despite the warnings of Jeremiah he too followed an anti-Babylonian policy and this led to the second siege and destruction of Jerusalem in 587 B.C.

As promised by Jeremiah, the Jews' exile was not to last long. Cyrus II united the Medes and Persians and began the great Persian empire. In 547 B.C. he defeated King Croseos of Lydia. He then turned his attention to the Greeks of Asia Minor and the Lycians and brought them under his control. He was then ready to turn against Babylon. Nebuchadnezzar had died in 562 B.C. and a period of instability followed: three kings in seven years. The last king, Nabonidus, was a strange personality. He instituted many reforms which made him unpopular with the temple hierarchy, but then he spent the last ten years of his reign in Tema in Arabia. Cyrus II appears to have been welcomed by some factions in Babylon. With the fall of Babylon, the Jews were free to return to their homeland, if they wished.

The first group of returning exiles were led by prince Sheshbazzar (Zerubbabel), possibly a son of King Jehoiachin. They returned to a devastated land. The south had been settled by Edomites and in the north there was a mixture of those not deported to Babylon and the peoples Nebuchadnezzar had settled there. Morale was at a low ebb. The Jews who remained in Babylon codified the law and it was from returning exiles like Nehemiah who rebuilt the walls of Jerusalem in fifty-two days and

Ezra who in 444 B.C. reestablished the covenant that the impetus for implementation of the Jewish theocracy came. During the domination of the Persian empire the Middle East had two centuries of peace, however it was not to last.

Alexander, the he-goat described in the book of Daniel, became king of Macedonia in 336 B.C. He inherited a war with Persia declared the previous year by the Greek confederacy. In 334 B.C. he crossed the Hellespont and defeated the Persians at Granicus and Issus. He destroyed Tyre (Zech. 9) and marched through Palestine to Egypt, where he was hailed as a liberator. Marching north again he re-defeated the Persians at Gaugamela in 331 B.C. Following this defeat the Persian emperor Darius III was murdered by his own men. Alexander continued campaigning but in India his men rebelled. He returned to Egypt where he died in 323 B.C.

After Alexander's death, there was a period of long and bloody warfare as his generals struggled for possession of the conquered territories. By 320 B.C. the empire was divided into three Hellenistic states: Macedonia, Egypt, and Asia. The main theme of the third century B.C. is the rivalry between the Selucids and Ptolemies. This is described/prophesied in Daniel 11. In both the Selucid and Ptolemaic kingdoms Greeks were the ruling class. Some Jews adopted the Greek language, including those of Alexandria where a translation of the scriptures (the Septuagint) into Greek was made. By 200 B.C. Palestine was under the Selucids. During this time the Hasidim emerged; these "pious ones" regarded the Greeks and hellenized Jews as enemies of Israel. In 175 B.C. Antiochus IV became the Selucid king. Jason, a hellenizing Jew of the Tobiad dynasty, with the king's approval seized the high priesthood from Onias. Three years later, Menelaus, another Tobiad was appointed high priest. He plundered the temple on the king's behalf and murdered Onias, resulting in riots. Antiochus returned to Jerusalem to suppress the disturbances. He massacred 80,000 people and decided to stamp out

Judaism. He forbade Sabbath observance and circumcision, and possession of the Torah became a capital offense. He converted the temple to Zeus worship.

Many Jews refused to yield and were executed, while others fled. Open rebellion broke out in 167–6 when the king's officials arrived at Modein. Mattathias with his five sons had fled there from Jerusalem to avoid conflict with the king; but when ordered, in his hometown, to sacrifice to the Greek gods he refused and killed the official and a Jew who was preparing to obey the Greek command. The Maccabaen rebellion had begun. Initially the Maccabees won several dramatic victories over the Greeks, defeating Apollinus, Seron, and Lysias. Lysias acted as intermediary between the king and the rebels, and by December 164 the temple was purified and religious freedom restored. The Hasmoian dynasty began with John Hyranus I (134–104 B.C.), grandson of Mattathis. He extended Jewish rule through Judea, Samaria, Idumea, the coastal plain and parts of the transjordan. The Jewish ruler clashed with the Pharisees who objected to his role as both secular ruler and high priest. At one point his son, Alexander Jannaeus (103–76 B.C.) executed eight hundred insurgents.

Internal Jewish conflicts lead to an invitation to Rome to act as a mediator in Jewish affairs. Alexander Janneaus was succeeded by his wife, Salome Alexandra (76–67 B.C.) who made peace with the Pharisees, but on her death her sons quarreled over who should rule. Hyrancus was deposed but returned with a foreign army to besiege Aristobulus II (67–62 B.C.). Both sides appealed to Rome. In 63 B.C. Pompey moved on Jerusalem and brought it under Roman control. Herod, appointed tetrarch by Anthony in 41 B.C., executed most of the surviving Hasmoneands in 37 B.C., when with a Roman army he secured control of Galilee. Even though Anthony was defeated by Octavius in 31 B.C., Herod was left in power in Galilee. He was a faithful servant of Rome and was hated by the Jews despite rebuilding the temple. He died in 4 B.C.

Jesus was born into a world dominated by the Roman empire. The precise date of his birth has been argued. On 12 August 3 B.C. Jupiter and Venus rose together to create a blazing light, and on 25 December 2 B.C. Jupiter was stationary in the heavens (having reached a point of orbital retrogression). So it is possible that he was born in 3 B.C. During Jesus lifetime he would have seen many crucifixions; following the census of 6 A.D. Judas led a military uprising and thousands were executed in the wake of its failure. Rome ruled with a heavy hand and found the Jews troublesome subjects. The hatred with which Rome was regarded is illustrated vividly in the gospels. The Jews longed for a savior. They expected a military leader—a new David—who would drive the Gentiles into the sea. It is recorded at one point that the multitudes decided to make Jesus king by force. All mankind is divided by the question: Is Jesus our savior? He declared himself to be the Son of God and that he came to seek and to save the lost. He healed the sick, raised the dead, exorcised demons, fed multitudes, and led a life free from sin. The Jewish religious leaders were terrified that as Jesus' ministry spread it would draw attention from the Roman authorities, who would then destroy their nation. They also hated him for his fiery denunciations of their love for money and exploitation of the masses' ignorance. The Herodians also feared him; if Jesus was the true king/messiah he would dethrone Herod. The Romans executed Jesus as a revolutionary; Pilate crucified him as "King of the Jews." Pilate was reluctant to execute Jesus and offered to free him, but his mentor, Serjanus, had recently been executed for treason and he could not risk a complaint to the emperor. When the Jewish authorities gently reminded him, "If you let this man go, you are no friend of Caesar. Anyone who claims to be a king opposes Caesar," he approved the execution of an innocent man. Tacitus records the crucifixion during the reign of Tiberius. The resurrection changed the course of history. Jesus' followers who had denied him days before, began to declare, "He is risen." Peter, who had denied Christ three times, advised the Sanhedrin, "Judge for yourselves whether we should obey God or man," and continued to preach despite his own imprisonment and the execution of James. Jesus appeared several times prior to his ascension, sometimes to individuals, sometimes to groups. He cooked dinner for the disciples in Galilee. He ate. He invited Thomas to put his fingers in the holes in his hands and his hand in his side. The appearances continued for a while, then he led his disciples to the mount of Olives and ascended into heaven.

The Book of Acts describes the growth of the early church. From the 120 disciples who met on the day of Pentecost the faith spread rapidly—3,000 being saved following Peters speech that same day! Philip converted the Ethiopian eunuch and Christianity spread to North Africa. Thriving Christian communities developed in Egypt and along the silk route. Even India is believed to have been evangelized by Thomas! With the conversion of the Roman, Cornelius, in Acts 10, the work began among the Gentiles. With his three missionary journeys, St. Paul, the apostle to the Gentiles, is largely responsible for spreading the good news throughout Asia Minor and Greece. The Book of Acts ends in A.D. 63 with Paul imprisoned in Rome.

The persecution of the church during the reign of Nero is recorded in Acts and in the epistles. Nero tried to blame the Christians for the burning of Rome in A.D. 64 and had several of them used as human torches and thrown to the hounds. Peter and Paul were both executed during Nero's reign. Meanwhile in A.D. 66 the great Jewish uprising began. In A.D. 66 Gessius Florus demanded money from the temple. The Jews mockingly took up a collection for the procurator. Florus came to Jerusalem to arrest the offenders and 3,000 people were killed in the subsequent riots. Civil war was also going on in Rome, where after Nero's suicide three emperors succeeded each other in rapid succession. Vespasian emerged as emperor and gave command of the war to Titus. In A.D. 70 Jerusalem fell to the Romans; the temple was destroyed and the city razed. Isolated pockets of resistance remained, but the Jewish state ceased to exist, until 1948 when Isaiah 66:8 was gloriously fulfilled and the Jewish nation was reborn.

GENESIS

Traditionally the book of Genesis, together with Exodus, Leviticus, Numbers and Deuteronomy was written by Moses, the great leader and prophet who lead Israel out of slavery in Egypt. The book of Joshua appears to have been compiled by the same editor, if so this would make it unlikely that Moses was the final editor of the Hextateuch (first six books of the Bible.) The final editor may well have been Ezra, or another post exile priest. The sources of these books are fourfold:

(1) The Yahwistic account from Judean oral tradition "J"
(2) The Eloheim account from Northern (Israel) oral tradition "E"
(3) The Deuteronomic account "D"
(4) The Priestly account "P"

Scholars believe that the J&E accounts were combined to unify the tribes after the exile of the northern tribes, then were again combined with D and finally with P. This would explain why some events are recorded twice from slightly different angles.

The book of Genesis (Genesis means beginnings) opens in magnificent poetry and glorious truth:

"In the beginning God created the heavens and the earth, and the earth was without form and void and darkness was upon the face of the deep and the spirit of God moved upon the waters and God said, 'Let there be light.' "

This truth, that God initiated the universe and man's existence, gives a purpose to our life and quiets our fears. God created the earth—it is no longer void and without form—for a purpose. All that exists was created by him and he is in ultimate control; we need not fear. God created both man and woman in his own image; he breathed life into them and regularized their relationship by instituting marriage. The Hebrew word used in Genesis 2:24 implies not just a physical bonding but a complete oneness, becoming one personality. The Bible is not puritanical; sex is good and was created by God for our enjoyment but is to be expressed as part of a total commitment in marriage. And marriage is validated because it originated in God.

Our world is plagued by sin. Our own greed, wrath, pride and lust causes nations to starve, murders, looting, rape, substance abuse, gossip and slander, and we cry out to God: why? Genesis explains the origin of sin. Sin does not begin (usually) with a conscious decision to defy God, to break moral laws or hurt others. It begins with looking at something that seems good, with a brushing aside or circumventing moral laws, justification of Godless activities to reach a desired goal. Like Adam, when we choose to do wrong something within us shies away and begins to hide from the light. C. S. Lewis wrote, "the penalty of sin is to have sinned." In the Eden account the immediate result was shame, fear, and loss of fellowship with both God and each other. The initial act of disobedience had a fearful penalty: man was driven from paradise and cursed. But when we reflect on the full consequences of disobedience we see the penalty was not too harsh. Every act has to be viewed in the light of eternity; each moment we are choosing to be more like God or moving further into the outer darkness where self is king and self gratification our only goal. In chapter 4, Cain murders his brother because of jealousy. His anger got out of hand and resulted in death. God warns Cain, "If you do not do right, sin is crouching at your door, it desires to have you, but you must master it." Like his father, Cain shows an unwillingness to admit his wrongdoing and tries to conceal the truth from God. He learns a lesson all men sooner or later learn: wrongdoing inevitably brings us face to face with God's judgement. Cain's descendants reach a point where they boast about murder. Lamech composes a song to commemorate his crime (Gen. 4:23–24). Evil was flourishing.

"The Lord saw how great man's wickedness on earth had become and that every inclination of the thoughts of his heart was evil all the time."

The great flood is described in chapters 6–8. Man's sin, and intermarriage with fallen angels, reached a point where God decided to wipe out mankind, sparing only Noah and his immediate family. Almost every nation has legends about this great flood. The encouraging thing about Noah is that he was not perfect. He was a real man with weaknesses like all men (drink). He was saved because he sought God—not because he was perfect. Chapter 11 describes the tower of Babel. It is an eternal symbol of man's arrogance and determination to become a god himself. The primary root of trouble in human history is human pride and self-aggrandizement, or more simply, selfishness.

Chapter 12 opens with the call of Abraham, ratified in chapter 17. Abraham is called to "walk before me and be blameless." He is promised that he will be a blessing to the whole earth; all who bless him will be blessed and all who curse him will be cursed. The covenant is established with Abraham and his descendants

"I have chosen him, so that he will direct his children and his household after him to keep the way of the Lord, by doing what is right and just," (Gen. 18:19). They are to be God's people. It is God himself who initiated the covenant of which circumcision was to be the sign and seal. God promised Abraham that his seed would be as numerous as the stars in heaven, as the sand itself, but Abraham's wife was barren. Sarah tried to help God out by giving her maid, Hagar, to Abraham as a second wife, but the Lord promised that Sarah would have a son. Sarah was well past child-bearing age and laughed, therefore, her son was called "Isaac," which means *laughter*.

Abraham's ultimate test came when God commanded him to sacrifice Isaac to him. The story has horrifying overtones. In Canaanite culture, child sacrifice was common. Was God not worth as much to Abraham as these pagan deities were to their followers? Abraham believed God wanted to prove that he was and wanted the sacrifice of his most treasured possession, the child of promise. Because of his intimate relationship/friendship with God and knowledge of God's loving and merciful character he was willing, despite his natural repugnance to obey. God stayed Abraham's hand and Abraham was blessed because of his total commitment and obedience. Abraham was unwilling to let his son marry a Canaanite woman, so he sent his servant back to his family in Haran to fetch a bride. The servant's prayer and successful mission are recorded in Genesis 24. Isaac had two sons, Jacob and Esau. It was through the younger son, Jacob, that the promise was to descend. Jacob supplanted Esau in the womb. He tricked Esau into giving him his birthright and finally, with his mother's conniving, tricked Isaac into giving him Esau's blessing. Despite this trickery it was God's will to bless Jacob. Esau had no regard for sacred things; he was a man careless and contemptible toward non-material things, a "profane" man. Esau had despised his birthright, selling it for a pot of stew. His own choices had made possible the success of Jacob's plot.

Esau was furious with Jacob and vowed to kill him, so Jacob with his father's blessing fled to Haran, to his mother's brother, Laban, with the secondary purpose of taking a wife. On his journey, he stopped at Bethel and there the Lord spoke to him in a dream and promised to watch over him and bring him back to that place. Jacob vowed to serve the Lord and instituted tithing (ch. 28:22). Jacob met and fell in love with his cousin Rachel and desired to marry her. He worked for Laban for seven years to pay her bride-price, but at the end of it her father tricked him and gave him her older sister Leah. Jacob then had to work another seven years for the woman he loved. From these two sisters and their handmaidens, Jacob had twelve sons (the patriarchs) and a daughter. Jacob served Laban again for flocks, and gradually acquired great wealth. Laban's sons became jealous of Jacob, so Jacob fled with his wives and children. Unfortunately Rachel stole her father's gods, so Laban pursued them. God warned Laban in a dream not to harm Jacob, so the two parted peacefully after Jacob took an oath not to take any more wives. He returned to Canaan, fearful lest Esau still wanted revenge. Luckily Esau's nature was not to carry a grudge. He was willing to let bygones be bygones. In fact he was delighted to see his brother Jacob arrive safely at Shechem (Gen. 33:4).

Chapter 34 describes the violation of Jacob's daughter, Shechem's offer to marry her, and the cold blooded slaughter of his town by Jacob's sons. Chapter 35 describes the tragic death of Rachel in childbirth. The remainder of the book of Genesis is taken up with the story of Joseph. Joseph was the first son of Jacob's favorite wife Rachel and the most beloved of his sons. Joseph is sometimes called a prototype of Christ because of the nobleness and gentleness of his character and because through his suffering and later exaltation he saved his family and nation. Blessed and singled out by God for favor, Joseph had prophetic dreams. He thus incurred the jealousy and hatred of his brothers.

Moved by jealousy his brothers plotted his death. Reuben persuaded them not to kill him, so they sold him as a slave to
Midianite traders and persuaded Jacob a wild animal had killed
him. Joseph was sold to Potiphar, an official of Pharaoh.

> The Lord was with Joseph and he prospered. . . .
> when his master saw that the Lord was with him,
> and that the Lord gave him success in everything
> he did . . . Potiphar put him in charge of his house-
> hold and he entrusted to his care everything he
> owned . . . the Lord blessed the household of the
> Egyptian because of Joseph.

Joseph did not hurl recriminations at God but accepted that this
was God's will, even though it seemed to contradict the promises
made in his dreams. Because he held fast to his faith, God blessed
him. However his trials were not over. Potiphar's wife desired
him, yet Joseph repulsed her advances and so she accused him of
attempting to rape her. Joseph was thrown into prison. There
Joseph found favor with the warden and became a trustee! In
prison he met Pharaoh's butler and baker; both men had incurred
Pharaoh's wrath and were imprisoned. Joseph served them. Both
men had prophetic dreams which they could not interpret. Joseph
said, "Do not interpretations belong to God? Tell me them I pray
you."

Joseph interpreted their dreams: the chief butler was to be
restored to his position, the unfortunate baker hanged. Joseph's
predictions proved true, but the butler forgot Joseph until two
years later when Pharaoh also had troubling prophetic dreams. He
dreamed seven sleek and fat cows were eaten by seven ill favored
lean cows and seven full ears of corn were eaten by seven thin
ears. Pharaoh was perplexed and distressed; he knew some calamity was foretold, but what? He called for the magicians and wise

men to interpret and they proved unable to do so. Only an understanding given by God can interpret the realities of today and tomorrow. Pharaoh's butler finally remembered Joseph and told Pharaoh about the Hebrew slave who correctly interpreted dreams. Pharaoh promptly sent for Joseph. Joseph told Pharaoh that God sent the dreams and God would give the interpretation: "Behold there come seven years of great plenty throughout all the land of Egypt: And after them arise seven years of famine; and all the plenty shall be forgotten in the land of Egypt. . . ." Joseph was not merely a visionary; he was able to offer practical suggestions: "Let Pharaoh look out a man discreet and wise and set him over the land of Egypt . . . let him appoint officers over the land and take up the fifth part of the land of Egypt in the seven plenteous years . . . lay up corn." Pharaoh recognized in Joseph both spiritual and practical power and appointed Joseph Grand Vizier. The seven years of plenty were, as predicted, followed by famine. There was famine in Canaan also and Jacob ordered his sons to go to Egypt to buy corn.

Joseph recognized his brothers, but they failed to recognize him. Joseph did not make himself known to them. Originally he imprisoned them for three days, then he released them ordering them not to return without Benjamin (Rachel's second son and Joseph's only full brother). As the famine lasted seven years, the brothers had to return later, with Benjamin. Joseph decided to test them to see if any change of heart had occurred. He bade them dine with him, but then "framed" Benjamin with the theft of his silver cup. When his brothers were dragged before him for judgement, Judah begged Joseph to have mercy upon Benjamin. Benjamin was the only son of his mother living, the child of Jacob's old age. Jacob would die of sorrow if any harm befell the lad. Judah, who was responsible for selling Joseph into slavery, now offered to become a slave that Benjamin may go free. Joseph could no longer control himself, he sent out the servants and

25

revealed himself to his brothers. His brethren were dismayed, but Joseph urged them, "Be not grieved, nor angry with yourselves, that ye sold me hither, for God did send me before you to preserve life." Joseph looked beyond the wrong done to him and urged his brothers to do likewise. He saw that the whole of his life had been shaped by God. God brought him to this place with his wisdom to be the savior of Egypt and his family. God's choice—not man's—determined his fate. His faith in God brought him safely through slavery and wrongful imprisonment, and now his ability to forgive was to lead to his family's preservation in famine. Joseph urged his father to settle in Egypt. Genesis 47 describes how he broke the power of the Egyptian nobility and how people sold themselves to Pharaoh for corn. Genesis closes with the death of Joseph and his prophecy that God will bring his people back to Canaan, as well as his exacting of a promise from his kinsmen that they will bring his bones back to the homeland.

EXODUS

Exodus is the second book of the Torah. Like Genesis it is drawn from four oral traditions, J E P & D. The title "Exodus" comes from the Septuagint scriptures (the Greek translation of the Old Testament) and implies the marching out en masse of a large company. The Hebrew Bible titles it "The Name Of," as the book opens with a genealogy of the Israelites who migrated to Egypt with Jacob.

Scholars debate exactly when the events described in Exodus occurred. The severe oppression of the Israelites began after the expulsion of the semitic Hykos kings. The eighteenth dynasty forced subject peoples to build pharaoh's great treasure cities and tombs. Some scholars believe that Thutmose III (1483–1450 B.C.) was the pharaoh of the oppression and Amenhotep II (1450–1423 B.C.) was the pharaoh of the exodus. Others, including Hollywood, in the great epic The Ten Commandments believe Seti I (1317–1301 B.C.) to be the pharaoh of the oppression and Rameses II (1301–1234 B.C.) to be the pharaoh of the Exodus. Egyptian historians would not record anything as degrading as the defeat of the gods of Egypt, so the fact that they do not record Israel's escape is hardly surprising. By 1230 B.C. the Israelites are documented as inhabiting Palestine. And by 1200 B.C.—in temporary alliance with the Philistines—they attacked Egypt.

The book of Exodus does more than record the enslavement of Israel and their deliverance; it shows God's victory over man's mightiest power, and describes how a gaggle of runaway slaves received the revelation of God's law and became—as the United States claims to be—"one nation under God."

The plagues inflicted on Egypt show how nature is used by God to fulfill his plan in man's destiny. Nearly all the plagues are "natural" and skeptics explain them away, as did pharaoh's magicians. Just as the men in the Book of Revelations harden their hearts and curse God when he inflicts judgement on them, pharaoh hardened his heart against Israel. The tenth plague, the death of the firstborn, broke his spirit and he agreed to let Israel go. The institution of the Passover is described in Exodus 12. Moses was instructed to put the blood of the passover lamb on the lintels of the doorways of the Israelites and the death angel would "passover" their dwellings. For Christians, Christ is our passover and we believe that his blood symbolically applied to our lives will ensure that we are spared God's judgmental wrath.

God led his people by a pillar of cloud (welcome shade from the desert heat) by day, and a pillar of fire (for light and heat) by night. Pharaoh changed his mind and decided to pursue the Israelites. Slaves were wealth and the wealth and power of Egypt was walking out of the land! Whether it was a serpent-tongued queen as in the movie, the Egyptian populace who were unwilling to work on the construction sites, or "The Lord who hardened pharaohs heart," pharaoh decided to pursue the Israelites. The promise given to Moses in chapter 14 is one in which beleaguered people of God have found solace in all generations: "Do not be afraid. Stand firm and you will see the deliverance the Lord will bring you today. The Egyptians you see today you will never see again. The Lord will fight for you; you need only to be still." The Lord instructed Moses to raise his staff and part the Red Sea. Moses did so. The sea parted enabling the Israelites to escape, and then closed in and drowned the pursuing Egyptians.

Some have argued that the Red Sea was the "Reed Sea" and the Israelites crossed in a couple of inches of water and mud. This does not match the Bible account: the wind blew the sea back all night long in Exodus 14. But those who choose to believe in the reed sea hypothesis have to explain how an army drowned in inches of water!

Chapter fifteen is a beautiful poem of victory. It is much more than a celebration over the death of Israel's enemies; it rejoices in the power, majesty and might of the living God:

Who among the Gods is like you O Lord?
Who is like you—majestic in holiness
Awesome in glory, working wonders?
You stretched out your right hand
and the earth swallowed them.
In your unfailing love you will lead
The people you have redeemed.
In your strength you will guide them
To your holy dwelling.

Chapters 16 and 17 deal with God's miraculous provision of food and water for his children in the wilderness. Chapter 18 describes the visit of Moses' father-in-law, Jethro, and the institution of a political form of government.

Chapter 20 is the famous Decalogue/Ten Commandments. In spite of its brevity and simplicity the code contains the essence of the spiritual life of Israel. It has become a world famous code, and until recently the Ten Commandments appeared in almost every U.S.A. classroom. The first four commandments deal with our relationship with God and are spiritual commandments. The next six deal with our moral relationship with others. Any society truly obeying and revering these commandments will be stable; families will be unified and will enjoy spiritual and emotional well-being. Those who flout and defy them do so to their own demise.

Example: the rioting, looting, murder, and arson occurring in the "City of Angels" in late April and early May 1992.

God's promise if we obey his law is clear: "Worship the Lord your God, and his blessing will be on your food and water. I will take away sickness from among you, and none will miscarry or be barren in your land. I will give you a full life span," (Ex. 23:25). Several civil laws are instituted in the following chapters together with regulations for worship.

Ironically, while Moses was on Mt. Sinai, receiving the law from God, the people told Aaron they wanted images. Aaron made them a golden calf, similar to the sun bull worshiped in Egypt and the Baals of Canaan. Moses was ordered to "go down, because your people,whom you brought out of Egypt have become corrupt." YHWH decided to destroy Israel, but Moses acted as intercessor begging God to remember: the people were His children. For his name's sake and in keeping with the covenant, YHWH could not destroy Israel. Moses asked God to be true to himself and the Lord relented. This illustrates, together with Abraham's intercession for Sodom in Genesis 18, the power of prayer offered in faith. One man can change history.

Moses commanded those who were on the Lord's side to come to him. The tribe of Levi rallied to his side. The Levities executed 3,000 rebels that day. The following day Moses again interceded with the Lord on behalf of the people. Moses set up a tent of meeting and went back to Sinai where he received a second set of stone tablets. The remainder of this book details the building of the tabernacle, ark, table, lampstand and other items used in worship. The book ends in glory with the descent of the presence of the Most High upon the tabernacle. The Israelites are thus given the gift they had earlier tried to forge for themselves: the visible external symbol of God's living presence with them. "My presence will go with you and I will give you rest," (Ex. 33:14).

LEVITICUS

Leviticus means *pertaining to the Levities*. After reading the exciting and dramatic books of Genesis and Exodus, the third book of Moses may appear extremely arid and dry and perhaps even repulsive with its emphasis on blood-shedding. Leviticus is divided into five parts, each of which has a co-relation to Christianity:

1. Chs. 1–7 are a manual dealing with sacrifice and correspond to Worship.
2. Chs. 8–10 deal with the consecration of the priesthood and correspond to Ministry.
3. Chs. 11–15 are a code of ceremonial purity and correspond to National Consecration.
4. Ch. 16 explains the day of Atonement and corresponds accordingly to the Christian concept of Atonement.
5. Chs. 16–27 contain Holiness codes and correspond directly to Christian precepts of Holiness.

The final compilation of Leviticus probably took place in post exile days, but most of the rituals go back to the Mosaic Age.

Our repugnance for the blood sacrifices and the graphic descriptions of applying the blood and portioning of animals, may keep us from fully comprehending all that Leviticus has to teach. The idea of sacrificing animals seems to us barbaric, yet the collection plate of modern churches is not far removed from it spiritually. We must try to look beyond the gore and ask what a sacrifice meant to the Hebrews?

A sacrifice was a gift to God. It was an outward token of self-offering. Without this self-offering the outward offering was meaningless and unacceptable to God. The sacrifice was usually a blood sacrifice. Christians sing of the blood of the lamb and its purifying and restorative power, but to fully understand the importance of Jesus' shed blood we need some knowledge of what blood sacrifice meant to the Jews. Blood was believed to contain life, so when blood was poured out life itself was being poured out as a gift to God. (See Rom. 12:1–2.) The emphasis was on the gift of life to God not on the death of the bull or goat. It was a costly offering. The worshipper had to pick an animal without defect from his flock, probably his prize bull, his pride and joy. He laid his hands on its head and identified himself with it prior to the sacrifice. The sacrifice was usually expiatory in nature, to restore fellowship with God. As the blood poured out it spoke volumes to the worshipper's emotions and subconscious; he was in a symbolic way giving himself—his life to God to restore fellowship. He would "feel" forgiven in a way that Catholics may feel after a good confession or evangelical Christians may feel after an altar call to repent. The Hebrews knew that the blood of the bull did not take away the sin, but by bringing the offering they were asking God to come near to them, just as a guilty husband knows the flowers do not change his harsh actions or words, but they do symbolize his desire to restore harmony in the home.

There are some beautiful little highlights in the book of Leviticus. For example in chapter 6:13: "The fire must be kept burning on the altar." The fire symbolizes Israel's worship; the worship offered by the covenanted people must not be interrupted. In a similar way Roman Catholics and Episcopal churches keep a sacristy candle burning to symbolize the Lord's presence. In chapter 10 we see the death of Aaron's sons Nabad and Abihu for offering unauthorized fire before the Lord. The exact nature of their sin is obscure, but like Cain they offered what they wanted to, not what God desired. Aaron's patient endurance of his grief is almost superhuman. Chapters 11–15 contain laws of ceremonial purity. We should not skip blithely past them. Chapter 11 details clean and unclean foods. The foods listed as unclean are those that if improperly prepared can lead to serious illness. We know now as the Hebrews did not that blood is extremely contagious, so the drainage of blood before eating makes sense to us. Those of us with a weight or cholesterol problem know why we should not eat animal fat. Chapter 13 gives important health regulations to prevent the spread of leprosy. Had the sexual conduct laws of Chapter 18 been more carefully observed the twentieth century may have been spared horrifying epidemics of sexually transmitted disease.

Chapter 16 is important to Christians as Christ is our Atonement. Chapters 17–26 give various laws, many of them mercy laws, allowing slaves to rest on the Sabbath and allowing for their eventual emancipation. In view of the Canaanite practice of child sacrifice, chapters 18:21 and 20:3 are of interest: anyone sacrificing their children to Molech will themselves by put to death.

The key verses are Leviticus 20:7–8: "Consecrate yourselves and be holy, because I am the Lord your God. Keep my decrees and follow them. I am the Lord who makes you Holy."

NUMBERS

The Hebrew Bible calls Numbers "in the desert" because this book details Israel's time in the desert. The English title *Numbers* comes from the fact that this book contains the genealogies and numbering of the tribes.

Numbers deals with God's disciplining and purging Israel. His transforming them from being a "stiffnecked and rebellious people" to being "a people set apart, who do not consider themselves one of the nations," (ch. 23:10) of whom it may be said, "No misfortune is seen in Jacob, no misery observed in Israel. The Lord their God is with them; the shout of the King is among them," (ch. 23:21).

In chapters 13 and 14 we learn the awful power of the tongue. The spies bring back a report about the great power and size of the enemy; this caused the whole nation to become frightened and discouraged. Joshua and Caleb stood firm, Caleb asserting, "we should go up and take possession of the land for we can certainly do it." But the malcontents prevailed and the nation rebelled, threatening to stone Aaron and Moses and preparing to return to Egypt. Numbers is full of rebellion: the Levities rebel wanting more spiritual authority in chapter 16; Aaron and Miriam rebelled for a similar reason in chapter 12. The nation rebels through fear of surrounding nations in chapters 13 and 14 and then again by deciding to fight after God has turned from them and told them to turn into the desert. They rebelled again demanding water in chapter 20. Even Moses disobeyed God at Meribah Kadesh by striking the rock instead of merely speaking to it (ch. 20:11). The nation sins sexually (and idolatarously) with foreign women in chapter 25. Typical of the overall history of Israel each rebellion brings swift punishment which brings repentance.

The story of Balaam given in Numbers is very sad. This prophet heard from God. He refused Balak's (the Moabite king) entreaties to curse Israel, boldly stating, "Even if Balak gave me his palace filled with silver and gold I could not do anything great or small to go beyond the commandments of the Lord my God." To the king in person he said, "Must I not speak what the Lord puts in my mouth?" Yet in chapter 31:8 it is recorded that he was killed by Israel, and he had been the one to advise the Midianites to lure Israel to destruction through sexual immorality.

Numbers gives the history of Israel between Sinai and the plains of Moab, May 1444–February 1405 B.C., making clear both the divine origin and call of Israel.

DEUTERONOMY

Deuteronomy literally means *the second law*. The book of Deuteronomy, or the nucleus of it, is believed to have prompted the great reforms of King Josiah in 621 B.C.. It is the most quoted book of the Old Testament by the New Testament writers—eighty-three times—and it is from Deuteronomy that Jesus quoted during the wilderness temptations. Why then is Deuteronomy so significant? Deuteronomy contains the creed of the Hebrew faith. Israel is the chosen race, and because God chose Israel and saved her from slavery in Egypt she owes him fealty. Deuteronomy makes it clear that Israel's choice is between life and death (ch. 30:15–28). Obedience will bring victory over their enemies—no matter how numerous or strong—it will bring blessing upon the land itself so that crops will be abundant and both man and beast fertile. But disobedience and idolatry will lead to drought, exile and death. The whole history of Israel reflects this truth. The basic law is the Decalogue repeated in chapter 5. However, Deuteronomy demands not just slavish obedience, it demands the right attitude of mind and heart (ch. 6:4–6), the law is to be but an outward manifestation of the nations spiritual devotion to YHWH.

The command to show no mercy to the nations inhabiting Palestine (ch.7:1–3) is one that repels us. Many Christians and non-believers alike, compare "when the Lord has delivered them over to you and you have defeated them, then you must destroy them totally. Make no treaty with them and show them no mercy" with Christ's praying for his enemies on the cross and wonder if it is the same God. Reasons are given in Deuteronomy for this command:

1. Deut. 7:4 These nations will lead Israel astray into worship of false Gods.

2. Deut 9:4–5 These nations are wicked; they practiced child sacrifice, demon worship, shrine prostitutes, slavery and social injustices were rampant.

3. To fulfill Gods plan of redemption as promised to the Patriarchs. Conceivably some will argue that Canaan, an inhabited land, should not have been promised to Abraham. However in Genesis 15:16 we see that when the promise was made, God foreknew that the sin of the Amorites would have reached its peak and be ready for judgement at the same time as the nation of Israel needed a homeland.

Deuteronomy is the fifth book of Moses, the last book of the Torah. It closes with the appointment of Joshua as Moses successor, Moses' blessing of the tribes, and his death of Mount Nebo.

JOSHUA

Joshua means "salvation." The book of Joshua is the first of the great history books giving the Deuteronomical history of Israel; like the five books of the Torah its source materials are the "J" and "E," Judean "Yahwehist" and Israeli "Eloheiem" oral tradition. "D" the deuteronomic historical record and "P" the priestly record. Joshua also contains the personal chronicles of Joshua. It is generally believed that the historical books, Joshua to II Kings, were written by the same historian. They have a similar literary style and identical theology. The main theme of Joshua is that national well-being is dependent upon obedience to YHWH. The conquest of Canaan was not due to Israel's might or skill; victory was dependent upon obedience to God's commands. When Israel obeyed, God himself fought for her (ch. 1:5–8). God dried up the Jordan River to allow Israel to cross. God destroyed Jerico. (There is archeological evidence that the walls of Jerico fell c1400 B.C.). It was God who rained hail destroying Israel's enemies (ch. 10:11). God granted an unnaturally long day to allow Joshua to slaughter his enemies (10:12–15). Those who trust in God, like Caleb, find renewed strength and are victorious (ch. 14:1–14). Disobedience brought destruction and defeat: "The Israelites cannot stand before their enemies, they turn their backs and run because they have been made liable to destruction . . ." (ch. 7:12).

Due to one man's greed, Israel lost the strategic battle of Ai. Large portions of Joshua are given to describing the territories allotted to the tribes (chs. 15–19) and to the Levities (chs. 20–21). As instructed in Deuteronomy, the inhabitants were slaughtered. The book closes with Joshua's farewell speech and the renewal of the covenant at Shechem. Joshua's challenge to Israel is a question we too need to face: "Choose for yourselves this day whom you will serve, whether the Gods your forefathers served beyond the river, or the Gods of the Amorites in whose land you are living. But as for me and my household we will serve the Lord." Joshua's death is recorded as is interment of Joseph's bones.

JUDGES

The book of Judges concerns the period from the death of Joshua to the time of Samuel. It contains oral traditions dating from the twelfth and tenth centuries B.C. together with written versions of these traditions. The first compilation of the book may have been in the seventh century B.C. and the final compilation in the post exile period.

The book contains a series of cycles. The nation would slip into idol-worship; God would allow them to come under subjection to foreign powers; the people would repent and cry out to God who would then raise up a deliverer or "judge." The judge would restore national freedom, and during his reign true religion flourished. Upon his death the nation reverted to idol-worship and the cycle was repeated. The time frame covers from the death of Joshua in 1390 B.C. to approximately 1045 B.C. The judges were unusual and diverse characters who were military, political and spiritual rather than judicial leaders and many had very human failings. Gideon was a coward and doubted God, but the Lord used him to defeat the Midianites. Jepthah was an adventurer who sacrificed his only daughter, yet he was used to destroy the Ammonities. Samson's great weakness was women and an incredibly violent temper, yet the Lord used him to deliver Israel from the Philistines.

The Book of Judges contains several incredible accounts and reads like an adventure story. The morals of the period are often extremely questionable. Ehud and Jael use treachery; Samson frequents prostitutes; the Benjamites at Gibeah are given to sexual perversion similar to Sodom. Yet despite all this there is an underlying certainty that the Lord is God. At each major crises they seek him earnestly, particularly in dealing with the disgraceful episode at Gibeah (ch. 19). There is a deep seated conviction of right and wrong—different though it may be from our own—and men accept God's judgement on evil without whining or complaint. The closing verse adequately summarizes judges: "In those days there was no king in Israel: every man did that which was right in his own eyes."

RUTH

The Book of Ruth is set during the time of the judges c1150 B.C. and in the Septuagint it is included in Judges. The legend of Ruth survived in oral and written form some seven hundred years till the post-exile period when it was written in its final form. Ruth, a Moabite, was the great grandmother of King David. Her name has become synonymous with loyalty and unselfishness. Ruth married an Israelite, and on his death she followed Naomi, her mother-in-law, back to Israel. There she worked to support the aged widow, and her unselfish devotion and fortuitous circumstance brought her to the attention of Boaz, a relative of the dead man, who married her. This little book raises the question: In the face of Nehemiah and Ezra's dissolution of mixed marriages, if David had Moabite blood were they right? Racial purity is not a criteria for holiness.

I & II SAMUEL

Samuel means *asked of God*. Traditionally the two books of Samuel are attributed to the prophet Samuel, but he died halfway through I Samuel, so later authorship is certain. In the Septuagint I & II Samuel are included with I & II Kings to form the four books of Kingdoms. The books of Samuel come from several different sources, so narratives are repeated.

I Samuel covers the period from the birth of Samuel in 1105 B.C. to the death of Saul in 1011 B.C. II Samuel covers the reign of David (1011–971 B.C.). Between I & II Samuel and I & II Kings the rise and fall of the Kingdom is described.

Samuel, like many other great men, was a miracle baby, born from an apparently barren woman. His father Elkanah had two wives, Peninnah and Hannah. Hannah was barren and cried unto the Lord for a child, promising him that in return she would give the child to the Lord. (Isaac, Joseph, Samson and John the Baptist also came from "barren" mothers, as though God delighted in showing his ability to surpass nature.) Samuel was taken to the temple and dedicated to the Lord. "In those days the word of the Lord was rare, there were not many visions." This was the age of judges, when every man did as he saw fit, and at this time spiritual leadership was at a low ebb. Eli, the high priest, was devoted to the Lord, but his sons "were wicked men, they had no regard for the Lord." Chapter 3 describes the call of Samuel. Unfortunately the first word of the Lord was doom for the house of Eli, Samuel's benefactor. The power of the Philistines was great and at this time they were oppressing Israel; they had captured the ark of the Lord in battle. On this same day Eli and his sons perished. In 1047 B.C. Samuel assembled Israel at Mizpah, for a time of national repentance. The Philistines attacked, but Samuel interceded for Israel and the Lord thundered against the Philistines who panicked and were routed . During Samuel's active ministry the Philistines were subdued, but when Samuel grew old his sons "did not walk in his ways." The elders of Israel came to Samuel and demanded a king like all the other nations. The Lord led Saul, son of Kish, to Samuel to be anointed king. Samuel's attitude to the establishment of the kingdom was mixed. He was deeply wounded at the apparent rejection of God and his authority, but at the same time accepted that centralization was necessary to hold Israel together against the encroachments of the Philistines and Ammonites. Saul was anointed king (1043 B.C.) and quickly proved his metal, decisively defeating Nahash the Ammonite at Jabesh Gilead. Though a mighty warrior "swifter than an eagle, stronger than a lion" according to his successor David, Saul's dynasty was due to be wiped out. Saul's son, Jonathan, defeated the Philistines in swift surprise attacks, but Saul was an impetuous and moody man and did not follow the Lord wholeheartedly. When Samuel's arrival was delayed at Gilgal, Saul usurped the priestly function and himself offered the sacrifice. He was unwilling to wipe out the Amalekites as commanded by YHWH, preferring to take plunder and keeping their king alive as his prisoner. Because of the disobedience, Samuel told him that the kingdom was going to a man after YHWH's own heart: David.

> Does the Lord delight in burnt offerings and sacrifices as much as in obeying the voice of the Lord?
> To obey is better than sacrifice and to heed is better

than the fat of rams. For rebellion is like the sin of
divination and arrogance like the evil of idolatry.
Because you have rejected the word of the Lord He
has rejected you as king.

I Samuel 15:22–23

Nevertheless, under Saul the kingdom was becoming established,
so much so that the Philistines determined to wipe out this
threat! Assembling a vast army at Mt. Aphex they launched an
attack against Saul so overwhelming that Saul and his army had
no chance of victory. Saul, his sons and the Israelite army were
wiped out at Mt. Giboa. So closes the first book of Samuel.

The second book opens with David, Saul's successor, being
anointed by Samuel after Saul's disobedience at Gilgal. Though
anointed and knowing he was rightfully king, David did not
attempt to overthrow Saul, instead he entered Saul's service and
quickly rose to prominence. He slew Goliath the Philistine giant
and the crowds sang of him, "Saul has slain his thousands and
David his tens of thousands." Saul became jealous of David and
several times sought to slay him. David refused to retaliate. "The
Lord delivered you into my hands today, but I would not lay a
hand on the Lord's anointed. As surely as I valued your life today,
so may the Lord value my life and deliver me from all trouble."
Now Saul lay dead and the throne lay open. David did not rejoice
in Saul and Jonathan's death. Chapter 1 of II Samuel records
David's lament for the death of Saul, and he praised the men of
Jabesh-Gilead who rescued the bodies of Saul and his sons. David
in fact ordered the death of the Amalekite who claimed to finish
Saul off and the execution of the men who murdered Saul's son
Ish-Bosheth. In 1004 B.C. David was anointed king over both
Israel and Judah. He then captured Jerusalem and made it his cap-
ital. The Philistines decided to move against David in full force
(II Sam. 5:17). David left the plan of battle to the Lord and

defeated them twice, at Baal Perazim and in the valley of Rephaim.

David's first priority was to bring the ark to Jerusalem and to start preparations to build a temple for YHWH (though the Lord told him not to; his son was to build the temple). Because David put the Lord first, God promised him, "Your house and your kingdom will endure forever before me, your throne will be established forever." David not only defeated and subdued the Philistines, he also defeated the Moabites, Edomites, Amalakites and extended the Judean sphere of influence over the Armenians. "The Lord gave David victory wherever he went." Unlike the usual oriental monarchs who destroyed all rivals, David asked, "Is there anyone still left of the house of Saul to whom I can show kindness for Jonathan's sake?" David befriended the lame son of Jonathan, Mephibosheth and restored his grandfather's possessions to him. The remainder of II Samuel is marred by David's domestic struggles. In chapter 11 we learn of David's adulterous relationship with Bathsheba. "In the spring, at the time when the kings go off to war, David sent Joab out with the king's men, and the whole Israelite army. They destroyed the Ammonites and besieged Rabbah but David remained in Jerusalem." Because David did not go to war he was idle in Jerusalem, and from the roof of the palace he saw a beautiful woman bathing. He sent for her, and they slept together. Unfortunately, Bathsheba was married to Uriah. She became pregnant with David's child. David tried to cover up, but when unable to do so he instructed Joab, "Put Uriah in the front line where the fighting is fiercest. Then withdraw from him so he will be struck down and die." Uriah was slain and David married his widow. Nathan the prophet came to David and told him a parable about a cruel rich man who killed a ewe lamb belonging to a poor man. David became indignant. Then Nathan said, "You are the man." He continued,

Out of your own household, I am going to bring calamity upon you. Before your very eyes I will take your wives and give them to one who is close to you, and he shall lie with your wives in broad daylight. You did it in secret, but I will do this thing in broad daylight.

II Samuel 12:11

David acknowledged his sin. In an attempt to change the Lord's mind about the fate of his and Bathsheba's son he fasted and spent several nights laying on the ground. The child died. From then on David's household was plagued. Ammon fell in love with his half-sister and raped her. David was furious but took no punitive action. Too aware of his own sexual misconduct David was unable to punish his sons. Tamar's brother Absalom "hated Ammon because he had disgraced his sister Tamar" and for two years this hatred smoldered and Absalom plotted his brothers death. After the murder of Ammon, Absalom fled. David mourned, but again took no disciplinary action. Joab, realizing David's sorrow, contrived to have Absalom returned. However Absalom resented David for his exile and felt wronged. At the end of four years Absalom went to Hebron—David's first capital— and began to build up his own court. David fled before Absalom. Ironically one of the most important conspirators was Ahitophel the Gilonite—Bathsheba's grandfather—who wanted to avenge his family honor. In the forest of Ephraim the battle between David's and Absalom's forces took place. Absalom was slain by Joab and his troops fled. David mourned his son. Kings closes with David's decision to number the fighting men and the consequent punishment, a plague, which David stayed by building an altar at the threshing floor of Araunah the Jebusite. "David built an altar to the Lord there and sacrificed burnt offerings and fellowship offerings. Then the Lord answered prayer on behalf of the land and the plague on Israel was stayed."

I & II KINGS

I & II Kings were written in c600 B.C. shortly after the death of
King Josiah of Judah. The books were heavily influenced by the
book of Deuteronomy (discovered in 621 B.C. in the temple
archives) and the reforms introduced by Josiah. They are concerned primarily with the splitting of the kingdom in two after
the death of Solomon and the idolatry of the Northern kingdom.
The books were edited and updated in 550 B.C..

Kings begin with an attempted coup by Adonijah which
David quickly suppressed and had Solomon crowned. Solomon's
reign, splendor, wealth and wisdom are glowingly described. With
the ascension of Solomon's son Rehoboam (931 B.C.) the
Kingdom split in two. The glory of Solomon's kingdom was largely financed by harsh taxation, the brunt of which fell on the
Northern Kingdom "the house of Joseph." Jeroboam was an official of Solomon's in charge of the forced labor gangs over Israel.
He led a revolt against the taxation imposed and built Sarera in
the hill country of Ephraim, but was forced to flee to Egypt until
Solomon's death.

Solomon's death saw the decline of the Davidic empire. This
can be linked directly to Solomon's idolatry and his building altars
to false gods: the Zidonian Astarte, the Ammonite Melek, the
Moabite Chemosh. Upon his death the northern tribes requested
his son Rehoboam to lighten the taxes. The young king foolishly

took consul from his courtiers rather than God and sent Adoniram to quell the disturbances. (Adoniram was in charge of the forced labor gangs which were largely responsible for the discontent.) Adoniram was stoned to death and open rebellion broke out. The northern tribes chose Jeroboam as King. Despite the fact that Jeroboam was originally anointed king by the prophet Abijah, he turned against God, fearing that if his subjects continued to worship at Jerusalem they would eventually give their allegiance back to Rehoboam. He built golden calves at Bethel and Dan. The setting up of the golden bulls at Bethel and Dan was in accordance with Syrian and Canaanite culture and also echoes back to Aaron's golden calf. For this sin Jeroboam was confronted by a prophet and warned that his kingdom would not endure (I Kings 13). When Jeroboam's son was ill he sent his wife to Abijah. He was again warned, "Thou hast done evil above all that were before thee: for thou hast gone and made thee other Gods . . . therefore, behold, I will bring evil upon the house of Jeroboam, and will cut off from Jeroboam every male."

Kings gives the chronological history of both Judah and Israel. The kings' reigns are dated from the reign of the king of the other kingdom and the main achievement of their reigns are noted. Rehoboam's reign marks a low point in the history of Judah. He allowed both "the high places" and sodomites. Shortly after his accession Judah was invaded by Shishak, Jeroboam's patron. Edom also revolted against him. His son Abijam reigned only three years and was succeeded by Asa. Asa was a loyal follower of YHWH; he banished the sodomites and displaced the queenmother for idol worship. It was during Asa's reign that the dynasty of Jeroboam came to a bloody end. Jeroboam's son Nebat was murdered by Baasa. Baasa continued the practice of local shrine worship. He too was warned by Hananai but failed to repent, and his son Elah was murdered by Zimri. Zimri ruled only seven days before Omri seized the throne. A familiar theme throughout the book of Kings pertaining to the Northern dynasties is "For his sins which he sinned in doing evil in the sight of the Lord, in walking in the way of Jeroboam and his sin." The Northern dynasties for political reasons worshiped the calves at Bethel and Dan and so were under YHWH's curse. The house of Judah for the most part remained faithful to YHWH, and up till the Babylonian exile their kings were descendants of David.

King Rehoboam was followed by three kings who remained true to YHWH and even won battles against numerous odds through trusting in the Lord. The book of Kings follows closely the fortunes of the Northern Kingdom under Omri's son Ahab (874–853 B.C.). Ahab allied himself with the Phoenicians by marrying Jezebel of Sidon. The wealth of Israel was greatly increased, but the worship of Baal also spread. The prophet Elijah was active during Ahab's reign. He proclaimed a drought, after three years of which he challenged Jezebel's prophets to meet him at Mt. Carmel. There he issued his famous challenge: "How long halt ye between two opinions? If the Lord is God, follow him but if Baal, then follow him." Both parties selected a bullock and called on their God to answer. The prophets of Baal were unsuccessful but the Lord answered Elijah by consuming the bullock—drenched several times—whole. Elijah slaughtered the priests of Baal. The fire consumed the sacrifice and his fearless stand converted many Israelites. Ahab remained unrepentant despite the Lord giving him a great victory over the Armenians. Ahab wanted the vineyard of Naboth, so Jezebel "framed" Naboth; she had him falsely accused of blasphemy and stoned to death. For this judicial murder Elijah prophesied the destruction of Ahab's dynasty. Ahab himself was to perish at the battle of Ramoth Gilead. Allied to Jehoshaphat of Judah, he marched against the Armenians despite Micaiah's warning. He died of wounds received in battle and was succeeded by his son Ahaziah.

II Kings opens with Ahab's death and the revolt of Moab. King Ahaziah fell through a window and was sick. He sent messengers to Baalzebub, god of Ekron, to know if he would recover. Elijah met the messengers and informed them that the king's death was certain and then went personally to the king and pronounced his doom. The king had no son and so was succeeded by his brother Jehoram. Jehoram renewed the alliance with Jehoshaphat and they united against Moab. Jehoshaphat insisted on consulting the Lord (via Elisha), so the Lord granted victory to the Judah-Israel alliance. Elisha's powerful ministry is recounted. He raised the dead son of the Shunammite and healed Namaan of leprosy. At one time he captured the whole Syrian army. Jehoshaphat was succeeded by Jehoram, during whose reign Edom revolted. Jehoram was succeeded by Ahaziah. Ahaziah was related by marriage to the house of Ahab and went to visit Joram of Israel. It was at this time that Jehu led a coup against Jerom and wiped out all the Omrid dynasty. He killed Ahaziah of Judah at the same time (this was partly to secure the succession of his own family and partly to prevent a blood feud). Jehu then assembled all the Baal worshippers and slaughtered them, but did not return to worshipping YHWH.

In Judah, on hearing of her son's death, Athaliah murdered all the royal princes with the exception of Joash, who was hidden by his sister. She seized the throne and reigned for six years (841-835 B.C.)

She made Baal worship—with all the attendant cruelties and immorality—the national religion. Her reign was short and she was deposed and executed by Jehoiada the high priest. Joash, the priests protege, began his reign well by restoring the temple but ended in failure and tragedy. This was partly due to the hostility of the princes and priests who resented his authority. Then followed the invasion of Hazael. This was seized upon by his opponents who murdered him and replaced him with his son Amaziah. In the twenty-third year of Joash, Jehoahaz Jehu's son began to reign. The story of his reign is one of unreserved gloom; Israel was under the domination of Syria. In his extremity Jehoahaz sought the Lord who had mercy on him. His son Jehoash revered Elisha and was present at the death of the prophet. Elisha told him to take a bow and strike the ground with it. The king struck the ground three times and Elisha promised him three victories over the Syrians. Hazeal died and Johoash recaptured all the territory Hazael had won.

Amaziah succeeded his father on the throne of Judah. He defeated the Edomites but foolishly decided to challenge Jehoahaz and was defeated. Like his father, he was overthrown in a palace coup.

In Israel, Jeroboam II succeeded Jehoash. He raised Israel to a pitch of materiel prosperity greater than any prior king. Israel's territory was enlarged and the kingdom enjoyed a time of wealth and peace. It was however, a time of moral decadence (see Amos). Zechariah, son of Jeroboam II, reigned for only six months in 747 B.C. In this year there were four kings of Israel, two of whom were murdered. This was a period of anarchy. In the last twenty-three years of the Kingdom of Israel there were six kings, five of whom seized the throne by murder and violence. Only Pekahiah succeeded to the throne peacefully, but he was murdered after only two years. The kingdom was reduced to an Assyrian vassalage during the reign of Menahem. In 735 B.C. Pekah seized the throne and together with Rezon of Damascus led a revolt against the Assyrians. Pekah and Rezon tried to force Ahaz of Judah to help them, but he appealed to Assyria for help. Pekah was murdered and succeeded by the last king of Israel, Hosea. Hosea began his reign as a loyal Assyrian vassal but later conspired with Egypt, and in 721 B.C. Sargon imprisoned him and deported 27,290 Israelite nobles and incorporated Samaria into the Assyrian province of Samariana.

Uzziah succeeded to the throne of Judah in 799 B.C.. He was a good king, but because of his pride in offering incense in the temple he was smitten with leprosy and forced to live in retirement while his son Jotham reigned as regent. Jotham followed the Lord. His son Ahaz, however "walked in the ways of the kings of Israel" even practicing child sacrifice. Rezin of Damascus and Pekah of Israel tried to force Ahaz into revolting against Assyrian domination, but Ahaz remained loyal to Assyria. This probably saved the kingdom of Judah. Ahaz was succeeded by the great King Hezekiah (715–686 B.C.). Hezekiah "trusted in the Lord the God of Israel, there was no one like him among all the kings of Judah, either before him or after him. He held fast to the Lord." Hezekiah sought to abolish all idolatry. He led a revolt against Assyria in 701 B.C. and was supported and encouraged by the prophet Isaiah. Jerusalem was miraculously spared from the Assyrians (see II Kings 19). Sennacherib withdrew from Jerusalem, returning to Nineveh were he was murdered in a palace coup.

Hezekiah was succeeded by Manasseh (696–641 B.C.). Manasseh's reign was totally under Assyrian domination. Manasseh kept Judah at peace by complete subservience to the Assyrians, regular payment of tribute and wholesale introduction of Assyrian religious cults. He is the only king of Judah likened to Ahab of Israel. Manasseh renewed child sacrifice, soothsaying, and necromancy. The fall of Judah is blamed on Manasseh's evil influence (II Kings 21:11–15). His son Amon ruled for only two years and was murdered. He was followed by King Josiah.

Josiah came to the throne in 638 B.C.. During his reign Jeremiah began his career (627 B.C.). Also Zephaniah (628–626 B.C.) and Habakkuk.

Josiah was one of Judah's noblest kings. He began the rebuilding of the temple, and it was during his reign that the book of Deuteronomy was discovered. This discovery became the signal for the most thorough period of repentance and renewal Judah had known. Josiah destroyed all idolatrous shrines and abolished pagan star worship. Then a great solemn feast of the Passover was celebrated. The original book of II Kings concluded here with Josiah abolishing every kind of heathen object in Judah and Jerusalem. Unfortunately, Josiah died before he was forty years old. Babylon had begun to assert her power in the days of Hezekiah. In 626 B.C. the Babylonian internal political struggles ended when Nabopolassar seized the throne. At the same time the great Assyrian emperor Ashurbanipal died. Babylonia began to attack the Assyrian empire, and in alliance with the Medes, destroyed Nineveh in 612 B.C. Pharaoh Neco II (610–595 B.C.) tried to help the Assyrians stand against the Babylonians and was marching to their aid when Josiah attacked him at Meggido. Josiah was killed and Judah fell under Egyptian domination. The Egyptian army and the remnants of the Assyrians were decisively defeated by the Babylonians at Carchemish in 605 B.C. Josiah's son Jehoahaz was taken captive by the Egyptians and replaced by Jehoiakim. Egyptian dominance was short lived. Nebuchadnezzar of Babylon, after defeating the Egyptians, invaded Palestine. Jehoiakim yielded and became a Babylonian vassal, but despite Jeremiah's warnings Jehoaiakim rebelled and was killed in a skirmish. He was an evil king and had filled Jerusalem with blood. He was succeeded by Jehoiachin. The young king inherited an impossible situation with the Babylonian army besieging Jerusalem. He surrendered and went into captivity in 597 B.C.

Zedekiah, the last king of Judah, tragically ignored Jeremiah's warnings and rebelled against Babylon. The second siege of Jerusalem in 587 B.C. led to the king's imprisonment, blinding, and the destruction of his family. The temple was destroyed and the Judean nobility went into captivity. Nebuchadnezzar made Gedaliah governor. Gedalaih sought by kindness and generosity to bring peace to the devastated land but he was treacherously slain by Ishmael. Despite all these tragedies, Kings ends on a hopeful note: Jehoiachin, after thirty-seven years of captivity, in 561 B.C. found himself released from prison and shown favor by the new King Amel-Marduk.

I & II CHRONICLES

After reading Samuel and Kings it is a surprise to find the book of Chronicles repeats much of what has just been read. The book of Chronicles was written 450–350 B.C. (possibly by Ezra) and looks at history from a philosophical perspective. It deals mainly with the Southern Kingdom and includes beautiful episodes not mentioned in Kings. The author presents a drama for reading and reflection. It is the Hebraic philosophy of history on a grand scale and drives home the point that whenever the King of Judah—irrespective of the size of his army—called on God, God heard and intervened. "The men of Judah were victorious because they relied on the Lord, the God of their fathers," (II Chron. 13:18). Ignoring God or allying themselves with idolaters brought disaster.

I Chronicles is a commentary on David and how God views David. In chapter 11 David is crowned as God's chosen king. In chapter 13 and 15 David's determination to restore the ark to its rightful place is seen. In chapter 17 David determines to build the temple. His victories over the neighboring heathen are also described together with his preparations for the building of the temple, which he is told will be built by his son. II Chronicles opens with Solomon's vision of God and his asking for wisdom. His building and dedication of the temple are described. Rehoboam's accession and the revolt of the northern tribes follows. The main theme is that right will triumph. In II Chronicles 13, Abijai when leading his men into battle against Jeroboam of Israel boasts,

As for us, the Lord is our God, and we have not forsaken him. The priests who serve the Lord are sons of Aaron . . . God is with us, he is our leader. His priests with their trumpets will sound the battle cry against you. Men of Israel, do not fight against the Lord, the God of your fathers for you will not succeed.

Jeroboam had planned an ambush for Judah, but when Judah realized the danger they cried out to God and God routed Jeroboam and Israel.

Asa when fighting the Cushites similarly prayed and the Cushites were destroyed. Jehoshaphat made an alliance with Ahab and was defeated at Ramoath-Gilead. However when faced with Moab and Ammon, he ordered his army to Praise God! While they were so doing the Lord destroyed their enemies. King Joash had the prophet Zedekiah murdered and was himself "judged," (killed in a palace coup the same year). Amaziah ignored the prophet sent to warn him against following the gods of Edom and suffered defeat in battle and assignation. Uzziah was victorious against the Philistines, but when he became proud and was unfaithful to the Lord was struck with leprosy. Jotham similarly conquered the Ammonites and "grew powerful because he walked steadfastly before the Lord his God," (II Chron. 27:6). Ahaz the evil king was defeated by both the Armenians and Pekah of Israel. Hezekiah's reign is glowingly described, together with his battle cry on facing the Assyrian invaders: "Be strong and courageous. Do not be afraid or discouraged because of the King of Assyria and the vast army with him. With him is only the army of flesh, but with us is the Lord our God to help us and to fight our battles," (II Chron. 32:7).

Josiah's reign is another high spot in Judean history. After two disastrous and idolatrous reigns this brilliant king restored the temple and reintroduced the Deuteronomic law. Unfortunately he lived in a time when great world empires were carving up the land, and his attempt to win Judean autonomy was doomed. He died at the battle of Meggido in 609 B.C. Despite the Babylonian invasion and the fall of Jerusalem, Chronicles ends on a note of bright and shining hope. Cyrus II released the Jews to return to Jerusalem and rebuild the temple (539 B.C.), and it is at this point that the book of Ezra opens.

EZRA AND NEHEMIAH

Ezra means *Yahweh Helps*; Nehemiah means *Comfort of Yahweh*.
Both the books of Ezra and Nehemiah are concerned with the
rebuilding of Jerusalem. Ezra and Nehemiah were at one point
part of the same book, and the compilation of both is attributed to
Ezra, who is also believed to have been the author of the books of
Chronicles. Ezra, the priest, was concerned primarily with religious reform while Nehemiah the governor was responsible for
rebuilding the walls of Jerusalem. The book of Ezra opens on a
note of glorious triumph: Cyrus King of Persia issued a decree in
539 B.C. allowing the Jews to return to Jerusalem and restored the
temple artifacts seized by Nebuchadnezzar to the Jewish exiles.
Early on though a sour note is sounded. The Samaritans, a mixture of Jews not carried into exile and the people settled in
Palestine by Nebuchadnezzar, ask Zerubbabel if they can help
rebuild the temple. They are harshly rebuffed, "You have no part
with us in building a temple to our God. We alone will build it for
the Lord, the God of Israel." The immediate effect of this was that
the surrounding people began to work against the Jews. In Ezra 4:6
they warned King Xerxes that Jerusalem is historically, "A rebellious city, troublesome to kings and provinces, a place of rebellion
from ancient times. That is why this city was destroyed." Xerxes
ordered the rebuilding to cease. Under the reign of Darius permission to recommence restoration was granted. In 458 B.C.

Artaxerxes I appointed Ezra to rebuild the temple in Jerusalem. Ezra revived the temple worship. In 445 B.C. Nehemiah, the king's cupbearer, was appointed as governor with permission to rebuild the walls of Jerusalem, which he achieved in fifty-two days, despite the opposition of Ammonites and Samaritans who were still offended by Ezra's rebuff. Nehemiah's workman had to build carrying a sword in one hand and a trowel in the other. Nehemiah had to guard against daytime surprises by his enemies at weak or isolated points and protect his men against surprise or deceit at night. While dealing with these external enemies Nehemiah also dealt with war profiteers who through usury were exploiting the poor. He publicly rebuked the offenders and made the nobles take a public oath no longer to charge usury. Nehemiah was an extraordinary leader, a man both of vision and courage. His memoirs were written in 432 B.C. and left in the temple archives as a memorial before God. Nehemiah was a eunuch—he had no children to carry on his name—his book assures his immortality. He was confident that with the guidance and support of God he could restore Israel. He regarded his work as a divine commission and his frequent prayers to God not to forget him are poignantly recorded.

In 444 B.C. on the Day of Atonement, Ezra reconfirmed the covenant. The Jews publicly confessed their sins and made a binding agreement to keep the covenant. The declaration was solemnly signed and sealed by the leaders of the people. They also pledged themselves by a curse and an oath to renounce mixed marriages, to observe the sabbath, and to contribute to the temple ritual.

The stance against foreigners and all things foreign is abhorrent to us in the twentieth century. The description of Nehemiah beating and pulling hair out of those who had married foreigners and driving away Joiada appears extreme. Ezra's lamentation and despair over mixed marriages seem sectarian and the dissolution of already extant marriages cruel. However, Israel and Judah had ended up enslaved by the Assyrians and later Babylonians because of faithlessness to YHWH; Ezra and Nehemiah were both desperately attempting to restore their nation and to prevent Jews lapsing back into idol worship. To Ezra all foreign contact presented a possibility of corruption, so to avoid divine displeasure and repetition of the destruction that had occurred he rejected all foreign influence. It was these arch conservatives who preserved Judaism during the years of Hellenistic rule. Judaism/Monotheism would have died out if not for the Hasidim.

ESTHER

Esther is one of the most beloved books of the Jewish people, though it is not quite so popular with Christian theologians. Esther links the community of Israel and the purpose of God with race and culture. As such it is at variance with New Testament Pauline theology where there is neither Jew nor Greek, male or female. In the story of Esther, Queen Vashti refused to answer the King's (Xerxes) summons to a royal banquet and was deposed. Esther was chosen from among the most beautiful girls of the empire to become Queen. In her favored position she was able to frustrate the plot of the Grand Vizier Hamaan to exterminate all the Jews of the Persian empire on the thirteenth day of Adar. Due to Esther's courage the tables turned and it was Hamaan who was executed. From that time on, the Jews celebrate Purim, or the feast of lots, as a feast of deliverance.

The main theme of the book of Esther is to show that though persecution will come, God will deliver Israel. To Jews it symbol-izes the miracle of Jewish survival. Some Rabbis give it preemi-nence over the prophets! It explains the origin of the feast of Purim, which is the only "worldly" Jewish holiday—a day that celebrates survival as a nation, not a religious holiday.

As Esther does not contain explicit religious or ethical teach-ing, it is a unique Old Testament book. Some theologians have tried to say the book is a historical romance, or a fable depicting the victory of the Babylonian gods Marduk and Ishtar over those of Elam (Humaan and Vashti). However, an undated cuneiform text refers to Mordecai as a high official at the court of Susa during the reign of Xerxes I (485–465 B.C.)

JOB

Job means *repentant one*. The authorship and precise date of this book are uncertain, though the language resembles sixth century B.C. literature. The book opens and closes in prose, but the bulk of the book consists of poetic debate between Job and his friends regarding the problem of why the innocent suffer.

Usually taken to be a book about patience, the book actually centers more on the problem of injustice. Job loses all his possessions and children and yet maintains his integrity. He loses his health and still refuses to curse God, though later in the book he cries, "God has wronged me and drawn his net around me," (ch. 19:6). "As surely as God lives who had denied me justice," (ch. 27:2).

Job and his friends start with the premise that God is all powerful and just, he blesses the good and repentant (ch. 11:13–19) but destroys the wicked (ch. 18:5). However their theology cannot cope with undeserved suffering. Job's friends are convinced Job must have sinned in order to be suffering so much, while Job fiercely maintains his integrity; he knows he is innocent (ch. 27:6). Job demands answers from heaven. Yet despite his almost heretical complaints about the injustice of the Almighty, he never doubts his existence or justice. Job simultaneously dreads God and longs for his presence. It is this need for communion with God that causes Job to cry out for a savior and to believe in an afterlife.

"I know that my redeemer lives, and that in the end he will stand upon the earth, and after my skin has been destroyed, yet in my flesh I will see God," (ch. 19:25). Job begs for a mediator (Christ in 9:33 and 16:18–21).

The book reaches a magnificent climax when God himself appears. However, God does not answer any of Job's questions. He demands that Job accept him as God and acknowledge his own humanity. For those of us who have followed the legalistic arguments preceding and accepted the premise that religion is a bargain—be humble, be moral, and be blessed—God's appearance seems cruel. He asks unanswerable questions and gives no comfort. But God is actually inviting Job to step forward out of legalism and into salvation. Job understands and accepts grace—free unmerited favor independent of man's righteousness. The point or major theme is that the man who has found true fellowship with God is rich even though he may have nothing left. Once Job repents however, God restores all the material things to him (in keeping with Christ's latter assertion that he who seeks to save his life will lose it but he who loses it for his sake will survive). It is in the Book of Job that Satan makes his first personal appearance since the garden of Eden. He appears as both accuser and destroyer in chapters 1 and 2.

PSALMS

The book of Psalms is a collection of religious songs listed at 150, though some original Psalms are broken in two, and several Psalms contain two or more originally independent songs. The English title *Psalms* comes from the Septuagint. The Hebrew Bible calls this book "praises" or "songs of praise." The Bible is the word of God to man; Psalms—one of the richest books in the Bible—contains the words of man to God. Every human emotion is captured in brilliant clarity and expressed to God. They personify man's dependence on and need of God.

Traditionally authorship of the Psalms is attributed to David, the sweet Psalmist of Israel (II Sam. 23:1), though others have contributed also. Some of the Psalms are obviously of the exile period. David is believed to have written Psalms 3–41, and most of the Psalms found in section 42–71 are Davidic in origin. Psalms 73–89 are from the Levite Worship in the temple and are attributed to Asaph and Korah. One Psalm each is ascribed to Moses, Solomon, Heman, and Ethan. Some of the Psalms appear to have been composed during the early post-exile period, fourth and fifth centuries B.C. So the Psalms cover a period of 1000 years from 1410–430 B.C. The final compilation of Psalms was between 400–200 B.C. The book of Maccabees accepts and quotes Psalms as scripture. Most of the Psalms were used for temple worship. Indeed the modern Jewish prayer book, the Siddur, uses all the

Psalms. Psalms are used extensively in the Roman Catholic liturgy and by the reformed church. John Calvin referred to the Psalms as "an anatomy of all the parts of the soul for their is not an emotion of which anyone can be conscious that is not here represented as in a mirror." St. Augustine wrote, "Oh, in what accents spake I unto thee, my God, when I read the Psalms of David, those faithful songs, and sounds of devotion." The Psalms contain prayers and pleas for help, thanksgivings and praise, awareness of God in nature and poetic reiteration of Israel's history. The underlying theology is that God is one. Righteousness, justice, mercy and faithfulness are part of him and are the basic principals of his government of the world (chs. 89:14, 97:20). God is gracious and forgiving (ch. 4:1). To be in communion with him is fullness of joy (chs. 16:11, 21:6). All of the Psalms are extremely rich, some more commonly quoted are: Psalm 1, an anonymous Psalm, which compares the fate of the godly and ungodly, of the godly man it is written, "he is like a tree planted by streams of water, which yields its fruit in season and whose leaf does not wither, whatever he does prospers." Of the wicked: "They are like chaff that the wind blows away."

The last verse in this little Psalm expresses the Hebrew conviction that the just man shall be blessed and the "wicked will perish." Life is seen as a covenant relationship with rewards and punishments according to our deeds.

Psalm 5,11, 34:7 and 91 see the Lord as protector of the righteous. He hears their prayer and delights in delivering them. Psalm 3:5–6 shows our true security—because of him we can "lie down and sleep because the Lord sustains me." The angel of the Lord encamps around those that fear him. When we recall that the angel of the Lord slew all the firstborn in Egypt in one night and 185,000 Assyrian soldiers in one night, how can we fear?

Psalm 10 shows the justice and mercy of God. Psalm 15 tells who may enter the Lord's presence: "He whose walk is blameless and who does what is righteous, who speaks the truth from his heart and has no slander on his tongue." Psalm 104:5–6 admonishes us to "enter his gates with thanksgiving and his courts with praise."

Psalm 23, the immortal Shepherds Psalm, is known and beloved by millions. Because the Lord is our Shepherd we shall not lack, there will never be a need that we will not have supplied. This relationship gives total security; all your needs will be met. In the valley of the shadow of death, the Lord will be with you, he will never leave or forsake you. Even when surrounded by enemies we can enjoy his bounteous provision without fear; our Shepherd is with us.

Psalms 8 and 149 instruct us in spiritual warfare. Psalm 8:2–3 reads: "From the lips of children and infants you have ordained praise because of your enemies and to silence the foe and avenger."

When we praise, no matter how weak or young or inexperienced, we silence the foe and avenger! Our praise shuts Satan up and invokes the presence of he who inhabits the praise of Israel (Ps. 22:3), to help against all the forces which oppose us. Psalm 149:6–8 throws more light on this concept. Through praise we bind the principalities and powers arrayed against us. In fact in praise we are taking our rightful place as coheirs with Christ and "carrying out the sentence written against them,"—the fallen angels.

Psalm 37 teaches us how to truly rest in God. "Do not fret" because of evil men. They flourish today, but their judgement is certain. "All sinners will be destroyed, the future of the wicked will be cut off." Trust in the Lord and you will be safe. Delight yourself in the Lord and he will give you the desires of your heart (ch. 37:4). This beautiful little verse cannot but excite us. But it is possible to take it out of context and bring ourselves much grief. It does not mean a spiritual equivalent of Aladdin's lamp! Some of our desires, if granted would do us far from good. We are to commit to him, yield to him, allow his will to become our will. When he moves our will and we desire what he desires, he will grant these desires because they will be for eternal, not just temporal good. (See John 15:7 and I John 5:14–15.) Commit your way to the Lord and he will bless you (see also Prov. 3:6). Rest in the Lord and wait patiently for him. The Lord is in control; you can trust him with all your problems.

Another beautiful assurance if given in verse 25: "I was young and now I am old. Yet I have never seen the righteous forsaken or their children begging bread."

God's provision is for you! and for your children. The righteous, by working diligently, have a good reputation "reference" which stands them in good stead in lean times.

Psalm 40 has inspired many hymn writers. It was originally two separate songs with verses 1–11 being a hymn of thanksgiving and rejoicing. Christians see the horrible pit as our sinful past and Christ as the rock of our salvation. For those who accept God, we are taken out of the horrible pit, set on a rock and given a plan and purpose (verse 5). Verse 6 compares the externals of religion with God's requirements: "Mine ears hast thou opened" (KJV). We need to hear God's voice; without this the externals of religion are meaningless.

Psalm 51 is David's cry to be cleansed and purified. David had just been confronted by Nathan regarding his relationship with Bathsheba and murder of her husband. He turned to God in repentant agony. "Create in me a pure heart, O God and renew a right spirit within me." He realized God demands broken and contrite hearts, that we must turn to God, trusting not in our own imagined merits, but on his mercy.

Psalm 67:5–6 gives a beautiful, but conditional promise: "May the people praise you, O God. May all the peoples praise you. Then the land will yield its harvest and our God, Our God, will bless us."

Perhaps the Californian drought is a symptom of spiritual drought7 At any event, this restates God's covenant relationship with his people. If we praise God, in deed and word, our land will yield its increase and Our God will bless us. The Psalm closes with a promise for the gentiles: "And all the ends of the earth will fear him."

Psalm 73 is beautiful. It shows how the godly man "almost slipped" because he envied the wicked's prosperity. But then he went into the sanctuary. "Then I understood their final destiny. Surely you place them on slippery ground. You cast them down to ruin. How suddenly they are swept away. . . ."

God's guidance and consul are promised. Verse 25 brings great comfort to the hurting soul, when feeling totally abandoned and unloved. "Whom have I in heaven but you? And earth has nothing I desire besides you. My flesh and my heart may fail. But God is the strength of my heart and my portion forever."

Having God, we have everything. In him all our needs are met. What on earth can compare to him7 Though our flesh wastes away there is something inside every believer, directly linked to him that grows rather than diminishes. He is truly the strength of our heart and our portion forever.

Psalm 90 is attributed to Moses, though scholars place it in the post-exile period. The theme is the eternity of God and the mortality of man. "From everlasting to everlasting you are God." Its heartfelt plea is "Teach us to number our days aright / That we may gain a heart of wisdom."

Psalm 103 expresses an individual's deep sense of gratitude to God for forgiveness and recovery from illness. This Psalm lets us perceive the truth "God is love." God is the one who "Crowns you with love and compassion, Who satisfies your desire with good things." It shows the magnitude of God's forgiveness (verses 3,9–12). God removes our guilt so far from us that we can never come near it. An interesting comment is given in verse 7: "He made known his ways to Moses, His deeds to the people of Israel." The people of Israel knew God's deeds, but Moses was more intimately connected to God; he knew his ways! Any stranger can observe our deeds, but our innermost thoughts, hopes and dreams only our true friends know. Oh to be like Moses and know his ways!

Psalm 104 is the beautiful nature Psalm reflecting God's glory in his creation. Not only the beauty of creation is exalted but God's wondrous provision. "The earth is satisfied by the fruit of his work."

Psalm 119 is the longest of the Psalms, God is addressed or referred to in every one of its 176 verses. This Psalm exalts the law of Israel. The date is probably sometime after Ezra. If we try to read this beautiful Psalm quickly we may find it monotonous or repetitive, but it contains some of the greatest spiritual truths imaginable. "How can a young man keep his ways pure? By living according to your word," (vs. 9). This is sound, if simple, advice reinforced in verse 11: "I have hidden your word in my heart that I may not sin against you." The Psalmist prays in verse 18 that the Lord will "Open my eyes that I may see / Wonderful things in your Law." He will run in the Lord's commands for they bring freedom, (vs. 32). True freedom does not lie in indulging our every whim. A life of self gratification does not bring true happiness. How many of us remember the morning after feeling? The Psalmists' freedom was to obey God and do his will; there is an exhilaration in this kind of freedom. H. W. Smith says in her book, *The Christians Secret of a Happy Life*, that perfect obedience would be perfect happiness if we had perfect trust in who we obeyed. If God is totally good and his will is "good, perfect and acceptable," then obeying him is our best possible course of action! This is what the Psalmist recommends: "Your laws are my delight; they are my counselors." Furthermore, "Your word is a lamp to my feet and a light for my path." If we fully trust and obey God's word we never need to walk in darkness. We just need to take the next step in obedience to his word.

Psalm 138:8 says, "The Lord will fulfill his purpose for me, Your love, O Lord endures forever." God has a purpose for each of us. No matter how hopeless our situation seems, God guarantees that he will fulfill his purpose in our life.

All of the Psalms are valuable, all inspiring. The more you read them the more you will get from them. The yearnings of man for God, and the reassurance he receives from God are invaluable aids for our personal devotions.

PROVERBS

The first word of Proverbs, *Mashle*, is translated as Proverbs. Some early Christian writers called it "wisdom." Most of the book is pre-exilic, and by tradition is ascribed to Solomon. The final composition took place around 400 B.C. The primary purpose of Proverbs is to teach wisdom (ch. 1:2). It is directed to the young and inexperienced (ch. 1:4), but also to instruct the wise (verse 5). Wisdom comes from God and is directed to God; the fear of the Lord is the beginning of Knowledge (ch. 1:7). It brings tangible benefits: "Whoever listens to me will live in safety and be at ease without fear or harm." Israel's cultural life was influenced by prophets, priests, and wise men. The wise men obtained their wisdom not from creed or supernatural revelation but from human experience. The wise men thought/mediated privately and gave advice in the city gate and in private. They formed schools and academies, but after the Maccabean struggle the anti-Hellenistic movement crushed them. Solomon was the chief wise man (I Kings 4:29–34). The main teaching of Proverbs is given in chapter 3, verses 5–10. Trust in the Lord brings guidance, health and material prosperity.

Other important teachings concern:

Adultery, it leads to death (chs. 5, 6:20–29,7:27).

Work, should be approached diligently (chs. 6:6–8, 10:4, 12:11, 14:23, 18:9). "Lazy hands make a man poor but diligent hands bring wealth," (ch. 10:4). "One who is slack in his work is brother to one who destroys," (ch. 18:9).

The Tongue, guard it well; it has the power of life and death (chs. 10:19, 20–21, 32; 11:11; 12:13–14, 18, 19; 13:3, 15:1–2, 18:6, 21).

True Wealth, chapter 10 verse 22: "The blessing of the Lord brings wealth and he adds no trouble to it." Also chapters 11:4, 11:28, 13:21, 15:16.

The Poor: "Blessed is he who is kind to the needy," (ch. 14:21). "He who is kind to the poor lends to the Lord and he will reward him," (ch. 19:17). "He who gives to the poor will lack nothing but he who closes his eyes to them receives many curses," (ch. 25:27). See also chapters 10:31, 22:9, 28:8, 31:20.

A beautiful model prayer is found in the prayer of Agur, chapter 30:7–9, and the perfect wife is described in chapter 31.

ECCLESIASTES

The title means one who convokes an assembly, but this book is a treatise on the meaninglessness of life: "Meaningless! Meaningless!" says the Teacher, "Everything is meaningless." Attributed to Solomon, it may have been written late in his reign c935 B.C. The teacher did not believe in eternal life, therefore the great building projects and possessions he acquired, even pleasure seeking and wisdom are meaningless; he will die and they will go to his successor. It is "meaningless, a chasing after the wind" for "like the fool the wise man must die." He acknowledges that God has a plan for man's life, but it brings him no comfort. "He has also set eternity in the hearts of man; yet they cannot fathom what God has done from beginning from to end." His advice is: "A man can do nothing better than to eat and drink and find satisfaction in his work." This rather dismal little book closes with sage advice: "Fear God and keep his commandments, for this is the whole duty of man."

SONG OF SONGS

Traditionally the Songs of Songs is attributed to King Solomon, possibly a wedding ode to celebrate his marriage to Pharaoh's daughter. It is a glorious, if somewhat erotic, love poem. It is included in the Hebrew writings where it is believed to symbolize the love between YHWH and Israel. Christians usually see it as reflecting the love between Christ the bridegroom, and the church his bride. Scholars have argued about the poems significance, some feeling it is a collection of Judean wedding songs, some seeing underlying influences of fertility cults. But whichever view we take of it, it is a glorious celebration of the joys of passionate physical love, which is but a reflection of the everlasting love of God. Physical love at its peak sees the adored object as everything and loses all pride in self, so are we called to love God with glorious self abandon!

Love is seen as a triumphant force, stronger than death, and impossible to destroy. The climax of the poem is reached in chapter 8:6–7:

Love is as strong as death
Its jealousy as unyielding as the grave
It burns like blazing fire
Like a mighty flame
Many waters cannot quench love

Rivers cannot wash it away
If one were to give
All the wealth of his house for love
It would be utterly scorned.

A New Testament parallel may be found in I Corinthians 13.

ISAIAH

The book of Isaiah is one of the most beautiful books ever written. It centers around the life and ministry of the prophet Isaiah, who was active during the reigns of four Judean kings: Uzziah, Jotham, Ahaz, and Hezekiah. Several autobiographical excerpts highlight the prophet's personality and allow us to view the wrath and terror of the Assyrian empire firsthand. Much more than a description of Hezekiah's defiance of Assyria—trust in the living God and subsequent deliverance—the book allows us to share Isaiah's vision of God. The call of Isaiah is vividly described in chapter 6. While attending the funeral rites for King Uzziah, Isaiah saw beyond the liturgy and glimpsed into heaven itself. Awestricken, the prophet looks upon the Lord—high and exalted—and sees the seraphs worshipping him. Isaiah is immediately aware of his own sin and the sin of his nation and cries, "Woe to me! I am ruined! For I am a man of unclean lips and I live among a people of unclean lips!" This vision of the Lord's holiness never left Isaiah. From then on he was to be continually aware of the Lord's presence, reality, and majesty; and this colored all his life. In the hour of Judah's peril, Isaiah was able to remind both Ahaz and Hezekiah of the unseen reality behind world history. Empires may rise and fall but only as God wills. In fact the Assyrians are merely a tool used to purge Israel of her sin, just as Cyrus is a tool to "comfort, comfort my people" in Second Isaiah. Both the prophet, and his kinsman King Hezekiah clearly saw the Lord in control and the primary shaper of history. The Assyrians have a mighty army but they have come against the Lord who made heaven and earth (ch. 37:14–18), and they are destroyed in one night (verse 36). History records the Assyrian invasion and the fact that their army withdrew abruptly from Jerusalem. Sennacherib's personal notes had boasted that he had Hezzekiah trapped as a bird in a cage, but it was the Assyrian emperor who was doomed.

Isaiah begins lamenting the rebellion of Israel against God. God is her father and the nation is pictured as rebellious children, laden with guilt, wallowing in corruption while God pleads with them to return. Isaiah is ruthless in denouncing external religion while the heart is hardened toward our fellow men, and the nation is told:

I have no pleasure
in the blood of bulls and lambs and goats,
When you come to appear before me
Who has asked this of you,
this trampling of my courts?
Stop bringing meaningless offerings!
I cannot bear your evil assemblies.

God will hide his face and demands that his people repent. If they do repent, "Though your sins are like scarlet, they shall be white as snow. Though they are crimson, they shall be white like wool."

The basic theme, not just of Isaiah but of most of the Old Testament, is given in chapter 1:19–20: "If you are willing and obedient, you will eat the best of the land. But if you resist and rebel, you will be devoured by the sword."

Isaiah demands total commitment to God, not just lip service (ch. 29:13). Social justice is demanded (ch. 10:1–2). Israel is urged to call upon the Lord for help, and not to seek foreign alliances (chs. 30–31). The Messiah is gloriously promised chapters 9; 11; 14; 25:6–10; 27. Despite God's judgement of evil, a remnant will be saved who will worship God in truth. The renewal of nature is also promised (ch. 11:6–9). All enmity between man and nature is ended; poisonous insects will no longer harm; the wolf, lion and leopard will no longer destroy other animals. The climax of first Isaiah is reached in the historical chapters 36–39. Hezzekiah's rebellion against the mighty Assyrian empire has apparently ended is disaster. The great fortress of Lachish has fallen and Sennacherib demands Hezekiah's surrender. He points that the gods of other nations have failed to save them. How can the Lord save Jerusalem? Egypt cannot help despite her promises, and the Israelis do not even have two thousand trained men to sit upon the horses the Assyrians mockingly offer to give them.

Hezekiah did not panic; he put on sackcloth—the garment of repentance—and went to the temple to pray:

> You alone are God over all the kingdoms of earth. You made heaven and earth. Give ear, O Lord, and hear, open your eyes O Lord, and see . . . O Lord our God deliver us from his hand so that all the kingdoms on earth may know that you alone, O Lord, are God.

Then he sent for Isaiah. God respected the king's trust in him:

> This is what the Lord says: Do not be afraid of what you have heard—those words with which the underlings of the King of Assyria have blasphemed me. Listen! I am going to put a spirit in him so that when he hears a certain report, he will return to his own country, and there I will have him cut down with the sword!

And in chapter 37 verse 36 we read that the Assyrian army lost 185,000 men in one night when the angel of the Lord smote them. Sennacherib himself was assassinated by his sons.

Chapter 40 begins the section of Isaiah known as *Second Isaiah*. It takes place in 539 B.C., when the Babylonian empire had fallen, and Cyrus the Persian permitted the exiles to return to Jerusalem. It opens on a note of reconciliation: "Comfort, Comfort my people, says your God. Speak tenderly to Jerusalem, and proclaim to her that her hard service has been completed, that her sin has been paid for."

The book is filled with great lyrical poetry, and the author is the first to see beyond Judaic thinking and realize that the suffering of the innocent can bring redemption. Universalism and redemption are the two main themes of this book: "The glory of the Lord will be revealed and all mankind together will see it."

"I will put my spirit on him and he will bring justice to the nations."

"Listen to me my people, hear me my nation: The law will go out from me, my justice will become a light for the nations."

Chapter 53 is the most moving messianic prophecy in the Old Testament and it describes the crucifixion. Jesus frequently quoted from Duetro-Isaiah illustrating how his suffering was to bring our salvation. Also in these chapters God's personal love for Israel and for us poured out: "The Lord comforts his people and will have compassion on his afflicted ones."

"Can a mother forget the baby at her breast and have no compassion on the child she has borne? Though she may forget I will not forget you! See I have engraved you on the palms of my hands."

"Though the mountains be shaken, and the hills removed, yet my unfailing love for you will not be shaken."

"Let the wicked forsake his way and the evil man his thoughts. Let him turn to the Lord, and he will have mercy on him, and to our God; for he will freely pardon."

Chapters 56–66, Third Isaiah, are thought to have been written by a disciple of Second Isaiah. The theme of universalism is continued, and the issues of corruption and moral depravity stressed as in First Isaiah: "Is not this the kind of fasting I have chosen to loose the chains of injustice and to untie the cords of the yoke, to set the oppressed free and to break every yoke?"

Third Isaiah closes with judgement on evildoers. The doctrine of hell is clearly stated in the closing verses but with promise for his servants: "As a mother comforts her child, so will I comfort you and you will be comforted over Jerusalem. When you see this your heart will rejoice and you will flourish like grass. The hand of the Lord will be made known to his servants."

The rebirth of Israel in 1948 is described in Isaiah 66:7–11.

JEREMIAH

Jeremiah means *Yahweh establishes*. Jeremiah is traditionally called the "weeping prophet" because his message was one of gloom and destruction. His ministry was during the tumultuous days leading up to the fall of the Judean kingdom. His message is primarily "Repent." The fall of the kingdom is inevitable. Judah must accept YHWH's judgement and eventually God will restore his people. Heavily influenced by the prophet Hosea, Jeremiah pictures Judah as committing adultery with foreign gods and warns that these "gods" will be unable to help when disaster strikes (Jer. 11:12). Because of these gods, disaster is sure and cannot be averted (verse 17).

Jeremiah was a reluctant prophet. His call is described in chapter 1:4–10. It is vastly different from the call of Isaiah. Isaiah eagerly cried out, "Here am I send Me." Jeremiah laments, "Ah, sovereign Lord I do not know how to speak. I am only a child." And indeed his ministry and vision are quite different. He is called upon to be a lonely voice speaking against popular opinion (ch. 1:18) and spends most of his ministry imprisoned and regarded as a traitor. His major message is, "As you have forsaken me and served foreign Gods in your own land so now you will serve foreigners in a land not your own," (ch. 5:19). Jeremiah's major speech—the temple oration at the crowning of Jehoiakim in 609 B.C.—earned his imprisonment and arraignment for treason.

Jeremiah warned, "I will thrust you from my presence, just as I did all your brothers, the people of Ephraim." The temple priests wanted Jeremiah stoned to death (the prophet Uriah who preached as Jeremiah did was killed at Jehoiakim's command), but the officials and people demanded that Jeremiah be spared. Jehoiakim continually rejected Jeremiah's advice and in 604 burned the scroll of Jeremiah's writings. Jeremiah and Baruch then went into hiding. Jeremiah experienced considerable frustration at being ignored (ch. 20:8), and several times his life was plotted against. King Zedekiah, though sympathetic to the prophet and having private audiences with him, imprisoned him and allowed his enemies to throw him into a cistern to die. (Later the King approved his rescue by Ebed-Melech the Ethiopian eunuch.) Even after Jeremiah's predictions came to pass and Zedekiah was blinded and taken captive by the Babylonians the people of Judah still refused to heed Jeremiah's warnings and accept Babylonian rule. After the murder of the Babylonian appointed Governor Gedaliah the army officers and all the people asked Jeremiah's advice. Jeremiah told them, "Do not be afraid of the King of Babylon . . . for I am with you to save you and deliver you from his hands. I will show you compassion so that he will have compassion on you and restore you to your land." However the remnant preferred to flee to Egypt and took the reluctant prophet prisoner with them. There despite his warnings they continued to worship the Queen of Heaven. Tradition has it that Jeremiah was stoned to death by his fellow exiles in Egypt.

Jeremiah's insistence on submitting to Babylonian authority as authority ordained by God made him a hated and despised figure. Much more popular was the false prophet Hananiah who promised that the Lord would break the Babylonian yoke. Their confrontation is described in chapter 28. Jeremiah not only called Hananiah a false prophet but warned that as he persuaded the nation to trust lies he would die, and within months Hananiah died. While Jeremiah's prophecies of doom are gloomy, his book contains messages of hope also: "The time is coming," declares the Lord, "when I will make a new covenant with the house of Israel and with the house of Judah. . . . I will put my law in their minds and write it on their hearts. I will be their God, and they will be my people," (Jer. 31:32–33).

In chapter 3:16 Jeremiah promises that the day will come when men no longer rely on external objects of worship—like the ark of the covenant—but will have a firsthand knowledge of God. And all nations together will gather in Jerusalem. Like earlier prophets Jeremiah was also concerned about social injustice and rebuked the nobles for enslaving the poor, (chs. 21:12; 22:2; 34:12f). Jeremiah promised that the exile would only last seventy years and this was fulfilled. In 539 B.C. Cyrus overran the Babylonian empire and permitted the Jewish exiles to return home. The book ends on a note of hope with the elevation of Jehoichin by Evil Merodach.

LAMENTATIONS

Traditionally written by the prophet Jeremiah, this little book laments the fall of Jerusalem and allows us to glimpse the anguish of the defeated nation. The people are starving, distraught, hopeless and terror filled: "With their own hands compassionate women have cooked their own children who became their food. . . . We get our bread at the risk of our lives because of the sword in the desert. Our skin is hot as an oven, feverish from hunger."

There are graphic descriptions of the dead lying in the street, survivors blindly groping through the ruins. The temple itself is defiled by pagans. Yet this is not purposeless suffering; the author knows the underlying cause:

> It happened because of the sins of the prophets and the iniquities of her priests. . . . Her foes have become her masters. Her enemies are at ease. The Lord has brought her grief because of her many sins. . . . My sins have been bound into a yoke by his hands they were woven together.

Despite this punishment, they are not left without hope. The prophet looks beyond their immediate pain and declares:

> Yet this I call to mind and therefore I have hope:
> Because of the Lords great love we are not consumed

for his compassions never fail. . . . Though he brings grief he will show compassion. So great is his unfailing love, for he does not willingly bring affliction or grief to the children of men.

The promise of restoration is grabbed (ch. 4:22). Like the book of Jeremiah this book laments sin, the effect of sin and its punishment, and looks beyond to God whose throne endures forever and who will restore his chosen.

EZEKIEL

Ezekiel means *God strengthens*. He prophesied to the Jewish exiles in Babylon between 593 and 570 B.C. Like Jeremiah he was called to preach to a rebellious nation: "I will make you as unyielding and hardhearted as they are. I will make your forehead like the hardest stone, harder than flint. Do not be afraid of them, or terrified by them though they are a rebellious house." God frequently refers to Ezekiel as "Son of man," implying that Ezekiel is the representative of man. This title Jesus later adopted for himself.

Ezekiel is called to be a watchman for Israel. He must speak as the Lord commands, warning God's people and individuals to repent. God stresses his concern for individuals, no longer will men pay for the sins of their fathers, but for their own sin. "Every living soul belongs to me, the father as well as the son, both alike belong to me. The soul who sins is the one who will die," (ch. 18:3, 20). "Do I take any pleasure in the death of the wicked? declares the sovereign Lord. Rather, am I not pleased when they turn from their ways and live," (ch. 18:23). Wicked men who repent are assured of forgiveness. Lest we despair of meeting God's standards he promises to institute a new covenant. And in chapter 11 verse 19, "I will give them an undivided heart and put a new spirit in them. I will remove from them their heart of stone and give them a heart of flesh." This is also promised in Ezekiel 36:26 and commanded in chapter 18 verse 21 wherein Ezekiel is looking forward to the indwelling of the spirit promised by Christ.

Ezekiel warns his people that continued rebellion will lead to further devastation (chs. 3 and 4). Jerusalem was besieged for a second time in 587 B.C. when Zedekiah was blinded and taken prisoner. His children were executed. (This was prophesied in chapter 12 verse 12.) That idolatry was still rampant among Israel despite the warnings of Isaiah, Jeremiah, Amos and Hosea is seen in chapters 9, 13, and 14. Ezekiel warned that the idolaters would be destroyed, though a remnant would be saved. Like Hosea and Jeremiah, Ezekiel accuses Israel of adultery (ch. 23). The reason Sodom was judged and destroyed may well give us reason to reflect on our own and our nation's spiritual status. "She and her daughters were arrogant, overfed, and unconcerned. They did not help the poor and needy. They were haughty and did detestable things before me," (ch. 11:49).

Babylon is pictured as God's sword of judgement. There is also a disturbing picture of Israel as the Valley of Dry Bones (written in 570 B.C. toward the close of Ezekiel's ministry). Israel's only hope for restoration is if the Lord will breath upon them. Ezekiel does not leave promises of restoration in never-never land. Chapters 40 on describe exactly how the temple is to be restored and institutes regulations for worship. There are some apocryphal chapters still awaiting fulfillment: the last great war with Gog and Magog (until recently interpreted as Russia) is prophesied in chapters 38 and 39. During the prophesy against the King of Tyre, Ezekiel sees beyond the proud monarch and discovers the controlling spirit behind him. He gazes at Lucifer:

> You were the model of perfection, full of wisdom and perfect in beauty. You were in Eden, the garden of God. Every precious stone adorned you, ruby, topaz, and emerald, cryolite, onyx, and jasper,

sapphire, turquoise, and beryl. . . . You were anointed as guardian cherub, for so I ordained you. You were on the holy mount of God, you walked among the fiery stones. You were blameless in your ways from the day you were created till wickedness was found in you. . . . I expelled you, O guardian cherub, from among the fiery stones. Your heart became proud on account of your beauty, and you corrupted your wisdom because of your splendor. So I threw you to earth. . . . I reduced you to ashes on the ground.

There are several prophecies against surrounding nations: Ammon, Edom, Moab, Philista and Tyre are all condemned for rejoicing over the destruction of Judah. Egypt is also condemned and told they will be overrun by Babylon. Babylon itself is also condemned. The promises of restoration and the institution of the new covenant glow like jewels in the midst of these dismal prophecies. The new covenant will not only restore Israel materially and spiritually, but will restore nature to its rightful condition, (ch. 34:25ff).

DANIEL

Daniel means *God is my judge*. The book of Daniel is a disputed book. Whether we accept it as a literal and historical book, or as a piece of apocalyptic writing, the events described took place between 605–536 B.C. The New American R.C. Bible introduces this book as "apocalyptic," written to encourage the persecuted Jews during the reign of Antiochus IV. Fundamentalists accept it as historic reality. Daniel and his three friends, carried into captivity by King Nebuchadnezzar, faced many trials and persecutions; they were willing to face death rather than commit idolatry. Shadrach, Meshach, and Abednego were told that unless they worshiped Nebuchadnezzar's golden image they would be thrown into the furnace. They replied, "If we are thrown into the blazing furnace, the God we serve is able to save us from it, and he will rescue us from your hand, O King. But even if he does not, we want you to know, O King we will not serve your gods or worship the image of gold you have set up," (Dan. 3:17). They were thrown into the furnace, but not a hair on their bodies was singed. And the son of God was seen in the furnace with them. Daniel was thrown into the lion's den but survived.

Throughout the book Daniel is gifted with both wisdom and prophecy. He foretells the kingdom of the Medes and Persians, the Greeks, Romans and even the EEC. He also foretells the antichrist. All these kingdoms are to be overthrown by the Son of

Man who establishes an everlasting dominion. Chapter 11 verse 36 and chapter 12 verse 13 deal with the antichrist and the end times. The book of Daniel assures us of God's ultimate triumph and is a call to wholehearted devotion and worship.

HOSEA

Hosea means *Salvation*. Hosea was one of the great eighth century B.C. prophets. His ministry began prior to the death of Jeroboam II in 746 B.C., but scholars debate the exact dates. He was influenced by Amos and it is likely that his work began toward the close of the earlier prophets. Like Amos, Hosea was a farmer. More about Hosea's domestic life is known than most of the prophets. He married Gomer who bore him three children: Jezreel, Not Loved, and Not My People. His marriage to a "woman of harlotries" symbolizes God's love for unfaithful Israel. The names of the children have prophetic implications. Jezreel symbolizes the fall of Jehu's dynasty. Not Loved and Not My People warn of the Lord's judgement and rejection of his people who have broken the covenant.

Hosea, like Amos, condemns social evil and injustice. His main theme, however, is condemnation of Israel's tendency to worship idols which he refers to as a spirit of prostitution. "A spirit of prostitution leads them astray. . . ." "A spirit of prostitution is in their heart." "You have been unfaithful to your God, you love the wages of a prostitute." Like St. Paul in Romans 1, he sees idol worshippers becoming as worthless as the image they serve. "When they came to Baal Poer, they consecrated themselves to that shameful idol and became as vile as the thing they loved," (ch. 9:10). These worthless images cannot help or serve Israel. The alliances with pagan nations lead to destruction and exile, (chs. 5:3; 7:11; 8:9).

The priests and religious leaders are strongly condemned. "As marauders lie in ambush for a man, so do bands of priests," (ch. 6:9). "My people are destroyed because they don't know me and it is all your fault you priests for you yourselves refuse to know me, therefore I refuse to recognize you as my priests," (ch. 4:6, Living Bible). And a return to true worship is urged. "I desire mercy not sacrifice, and acknowledgement of God rather than burnt offerings," (ch. 6:6). "You must return to your God, maintain love and justice and wait for your God always," (ch. 12:6). Chapter 14 describes the restoration of Israel when she repents and closes with a call to the wise to understand that "the ways of the Lord are right, the righteous walk in them but the rebellious stumble in them."

JOEL

Joel means *YHWH is God*. Scholars debate when the book of Joel was written. Some hold that it was written in 835 B.C. (pre-exile), while the Assyrians were a growing threat. The descriptions of the invasion of locusts matches what we know of the Assyrians: well disciplined and merciless. Joel could have foreseen the invasion of the Assyrians accurately. (Isaiah 1 describes the condition of Judah after their invasion and we can see similarities in the two accounts.) Other scholars believe it is a post-exile poem written c400 B.C. Whichever view we choose to take, the central theme is not the physical invasion of the locusts/Assyrians; it is that the locusts are a foretaste of the day of judgement (as well as being a judgement). Judah is called to repent. If true repentance occurs God will restore his favor:

> Put on sackcloth, O Priests, and mourn; wail you who minister before the altar. Come, spend the night in sackcloth you who minister before my God. . . . Return to the Lord your God, for his is gracious and compassionate, slow to anger and abounding in love and he relents from sending calamity.

The book of Joel is an optimistic book. It looks beyond the invasion to the Lord's showering favor on his returned people, then beyond that to the gift of the Holy Spirit. Peter quotes Joel 2:28 in his speech on the day of Pentecost. The final great day when the Lord will avenge his people is foretold in chapter 3.

AMOS

The book of Amos is one of the most entertaining and challenging books of the Old Testament. Written between 760–745 B.C. by Amos, it deals with the judgement passed on Israel (exile and captivity), the fairness of this judgement and the reasons for it. The key verse is chapter 3:2: "You only have I known of all the families of the earth; therefore will I punish you for all your iniquities."

Amos, the main character/speaker, was a herdsman/farmer, not a professional religious leader. He is the opposite of the priest Amaziah. Amaziah is rich, powerful, educated and has the ear of King Jeroboam II but is totally deaf toward God. Chapter 7:10–17 show the two: the poor man commissioned by God and the professional priest in sharp conflict. Amaziah does not want to hear about judgement. Contemptuously he orders Amos: "O thou seer. Go, flee thee away into the land of Judah and there eat bread and prophecy there, but prophecy not again anymore at Bethel, for it is the King's chapel, and it is the King's court."

The prophet proclaims his credentials: "I was no prophet, neither was I a prophet's son, but I was an herdsman and a gatherer of sycamore fruit: And the Lord took me as I followed the flock and the Lord said unto me, Go prophecy unto my people Israel. . . ." Then in verses 16 and 17 Amos pronounces a dire judgement on the priest.

The greatest lesson is that God's judgement is just and begins with his own people. Amos leads into his message by pronouncing judgement on the neighboring pagan nations. Damascus is judged for cruelty, Gaza and Tyre for practicing slavery, Edom and Moab for cruelty and lack of compassion on a defeated foe. The Israelites hated these pagan nations and are in total agreement with the prophet that they should be judged. Amos slowly moves closer to home. Judah the southern kingdom is judged. Judah had rejected the commandments of the Lord and followed false Gods. Then Amos hits home! Chapter 2:6–7:

> For three transgressions of Israel and for four, I will
> not turn away the punishment thereof because
> they sold the righteous for silver and the poor for a
> pair of shoes; That pant after the dust of the earth
> on the head of the poor, and turn aside the way of
> the meek: and a man and his father will go in unto
> the same maid, to profane my holy name.

So far Amos had carried his audience along with him; they agreed that the "sinful" pagans must be judged and now find they are confronted with their own sin! Amos is ruthless in pronouncing God's judgement on his externally pious people: "I hate I despise your feast days. . . . take thou away from me the noise of thy song for I will not hear the melody of thy violas. But let judgement run down as waters, and righteousness as a mighty stream," (ch. 5:21–24).

And in chapter 4:4:

> Come to Bethel and transgress, at Gilgal multiply
> transgressions and bring your sacrifice every morn-
> ing and your tithes every three years, and offer a
> sacrifice of thanksgiving with leaven and proclaim

and publish the freewill offerings for this liketh
you, o ye children of Israel.

Though Amos is pronouncing judgement on Israel for her sins,
hope is extended if true repentance occurs and the book ends on a
note of hope (ch 9:14–15). Continually throughout the book God
pleads, "Seek me and live."

A secondary and frightening lesson is that the Lord will eventually leave us if we continue to ignore his commands, (ch. 8:11).
Dishonest business dealing is condemned, (ch. 8:5). Hardhearted
complacency is condemned in chapters 4 and 6.

OBADIAH

Obadiah means *servant to YHWH*. This little book takes up only one chapter of the Bible. It is a lament for Esau/Edom who are being judged for "violence against your brother Jacob." As with a lot of the prophetic books, there is dispute about when it was written. If Obadiah was the faithful servant of YHWH mentioned in I Kings 18 who saved the prophets of the Lord from Jezebel, the book may be dated c840 B.C.

JONAH

Almost everyone knows the story of Jonah and the great fish. God told Jonah to warn the Ninevites that unless they repented they would be destroyed. Nineveh was the capital of the Assyrian empire and the Assyrians were famed for cruelty, so Jonah was reluctant to go. He fled from God and boarded a ship bound for Tarshish. The Lord caused a great storm. When Jonah was thrown overboard to quiet the storm, God caused him to be swallowed by a great fish. While inside the fish Jonah repented and the Lord caused the fish to vomit Jonah ashore, close to Nineveh. Jonah duly preached and the city repented. The prophet was furious and sat outside the city sulking because he felt foolish. God caused a vine to grow up to shelter him but the following day caused it to wither. Then he spoke to the hard hearted prophet:

> You have been concerned about this vine, though you did not tend it or make it grow. It sprang up overnight and died overnight. But Niveneh has more than a hundred and twenty thousand people. . . . should I not be concerned about that great city?

There are two views of this book. Fundamentalist accept the book as historic. The prophet Jonah, mentioned in II Kings 14:25 came from Goth Hepher and ministered during the reign of Jeroboam II.

This would date the book c785 B.C. Jesus accepted the book as literal (Mt. 12:39–41; Lk. 11:29–32). Some liberal theologians see the book as a parable, written in the post exile period 400–200 B.C., during which time the Jewish nationalism was at a fever pitch. Babylonian Jews, like Ezra and Nehemiah, forced the dissolution of interracial marriage and were intent on establishing a torah-based theocracy. These theologians believe that the book uses satire to illustrate God's mercy to all men and the fraudulent piety of sectarianism. Whichever view we take the key verse is Jonah 4:11. God is concerned about all men and has no desire to see them perish.

MICAH

Micah means *who is like God*. Micah was contemporary with Amos, Isaiah, and Hosea. He prophesied in Judah between 735–710 B.C. approximately. Like the others he foretells judgements/exile for sin: idolatry, greed and social injustice, unfair business practices, lies, encouragement of false prophets and discouragement of true prophets.

Restoration is promised in chapter 4 and the birth of the Messiah in Bethlehem is foretold in chapter 6. Micah stresses that sacrifice without repentance is useless and gives the Old Testament equivalent of the Golden Commandments: "He has shown you, O man, what is good, And what does the Lord require of you? To act justly and to love mercy and to walk humbly with thy God."

The book ends with declarations of hope and trust in God's mercy and forgiveness.

NAHUM

Nahum means *comfort*, but there is little of comfort in his prophecy. Like Jonah, the book of Nahum is addressed to the Assyrian Royal City of Nineveh. It is set c660 B.C.—120 years after Jonah's preaching. The city has returned to its former practices: "Woe to the city of blood, Full of plunder, never without victims . . . Who has not felt your endless cruelty."

Nahum's message is one of judgement. Nineveh is to be destroyed. "I will prepare your grave for you are vile." The fulfillment of this prophecy shook the ancient world. In 612 the great city of Nineveh fell to the Babylonians and by 605 the Assyrian Empire was itself destroyed.

HABAKKUK

Habakkuk means *one who embraces*. The prophet Habakkuk wrote between 608–605 B.C. during the death throes of the Assyrian Empire. Palestine was being swept through by both Egyptian and Babylonian armies. King Josiah had perished at Meggido in 609 B.C. Now the Hebrews were under Egyptian domination, sick and frightened as a nation. Habakkuk calls upon God, "Why do you tolerate wrong?" "The law is paralyzed, justice never prevails, the wicked hem in the righteous so that justice is perverted." The Lord warns Habakkuk that he is raising up Babylon "to sweep across the whole earth." Habakkuk accepts that the Lord has appointed the Babylonians to punish Judah for her sins, but the Babylonians are merciless and God cannot tolerate them forever. The Lord answers, giving timeless words of comfort. Just as the Assyrians are destroyed for their cruelty—the Babylonians trust in idols and their own strength—their bloodshedding will lead to their downfall: "Woe to him who builds a city with bloodshed and establishes a town by crime. . . . The nations exhaust themselves for nothing, for the earth will be filled with the knowledge of the glory of the Lord, as the waters cover the sea."

The book of Habakkuk closes with some of the greatest declarations of faith a man can make. Habakkuk looks across a devastated and starving land and then lifts his voice in exultant praise to God,

Though the fig tree does not bud and there are no grapes on the vines, though the olive crop fails and the fields produce no food, though there are no sheep in the pen and no cattle in the stalls. Yet I will rejoice in the Lord I will be joyful in God my savior.

No matter how awful our circumstances are, we can draw strength from these lines and look as did Habakkuk, to "the Sovereign Lord is my strength he makes my feet like the feet of a deer he enables me to go on the heights."

When we truly trust in God, no situation we face can destroy us, and through praise we shall be enabled to stand in his presence in victory.

ZEPHANIAH

Zephaniah means *YHWH has hidden*. Like Isaiah, Zephaniah was a prince, a second cousin to King Josiah. His book was written c626 B.C. It is a warning of judgement. Judah is still filled with idol worship (particularly to Molech). Jerusalem is steeped in oppression and treachery. Unless true repentance occurs judgement is certain. Surrounding pagan nations—Philistia, Moab, Amon and Cush—are to be destroyed with Assyria. The Lord warns of his purifying judgement. But after that is past, glorious restoration is promised: "The Lord your God is with you. He is mighty to save; He will take delight in you; He will quiet you with his love. He will rejoice over you with singing."

HAGGAI

Haggai means *festal*. His book contains only two chapters and was written in 520 B.C. to the exiles returning from Babylon. It is to encourage them to rebuild the temple *now*. The returning exiles were depressed by the Edomite invasion in the south and the presence of foreigners settled by Nebuchadnezzar. They had started work on the temple but on encountering opposition stopped. Now they faced failing crops and morale was low. Haggai reminds them that despite this they have managed to rebuild their own house and start their businesses. Now pay attention to God's house and his business. "You expected much, but, see, it turned out to be little. What you brought home I blew away. Why? declares the Lord Almighty. . . . Because of my house, which remains a ruin, while each of you is busy with his own house." Do not ever be too busy to put God first. When the priests and governor repent and recommence the work, Haggai promises the Lord's blessing.

ZECHARIAH

Zechariah means *God Remembers*. This book was written between February 519 and December 518 B.C. It resembles Haggai, encouraging the returning exiles. It is a truly beautiful book filled with God's love and concern for Judah and Jerusalem. The Jews are encouraged to rebuild the temple that the land may prosper (ch. 8:9–12). Some of the prophecies regarding the high priest Joshua appear not to have been fulfilled. However, it must be stressed that these prophecies were conditional promises: "This will happen if you diligently obey the Lord your God," (ch. 6:15).

The main teaching of the book is given in chapter 7:9: "Administer true justice, show mercy and compassion to one another. Do not oppress the widow, or the fatherless, the alien or the poor. In your hearts do not think evil of each other." There are prophecies against Israel's enemies but also a vision of the crucifixion (ch. 12:10–14). Then chapter 14 deals with the second coming. The Lord's enemies are gathered against Jerusalem and are destroyed by a fearful plague—which sounds like nuclear fallout—and the messiah descends on the mount of Olives with his holy ones, causing it to split. The river of life, described also in Revelations, flows from Jerusalem and the Lord begins his millennium reign.

MALACHI

Malachi means *my messenger*. The book of Malachi is the last book in the Old Testament. Written in approximately 450 B.C., it precedes Nehemiah's reforms. The people of Israel are rebuked for not honoring God; their offerings are made half-heartedly—blind, crippled, and diseased animals are offered. The Lord asks, "If I am a father, where is the honor due me? If I am a master where is the respect due to me?" As the offerings are made without reverence they are unacceptable and useless, (ch. 1:10). Malachi—though a devout Jew—looks beyond the physical to the spiritual condition of the people and in verse 11 receives a revelation: All honest worship, to whatever deity it may ostensibly be offered is really worship of the one true God and is accepted by him in the spirit in which it is offered. Malachi foresees the day when all nations will worship the one true God (ch. 1:11).

Chapter 2 verse 14 digresses to give the Lord's poignant instructions concerning divorce: "I hate divorce." This harkens back to Genesis 2:24 where man and woman become one in both flesh and spirit. Malachi quickly returns to his theme, Israel's attitude toward God. The Jews are warned they are robbing God by not tithing (ch. 3:10). If they will tithe the Lord will not only abundantly bless them, he will rebuke the destroyer (verse 11). Grumblings and murmurrings have been heard and the Lord assures the righteous that he will institute true justice and the wicked will be punished. The coming of John the Baptizer (Elijah) immediately before the messiah is foretold, and on this note of hope the Old Testament ends.

THE APOCRYHPHA

Some Old Testament books not accepted by either the Jews or reformed churches are accepted by the Roman Catholic Church.

ADDITIONS TO ESTHER: Mordecai's dream at the beginning of the book of Esther and his closing speech. These are included in the Greek version of the scroll, but not in the Hebrew. Only the Catholic Church accepts these later additions as equally canonical.

ADDITIONS TO DANIEL: Chapters 13 and 14, the legend of Susanna, Bel and the dragon. All are found only in the Greek version. They are short, edifying adventure stories.

THE BOOK OF TOBIT: Written early in the second century B.C., tells a romance between a penniless Tobiah, son of the devout Tobit, and Sarah, who has the misfortune to be the beloved of the demon Asmodeus. The angel Raphael intervenes to free Sarah from the demon's attentions and to heal Tobit of his blindness. It is an extremely enjoyable adventure tale.

THE BOOK OF JUDITH: Written at the end of the second century B.C., describes how the Lord used the beauty of Judith (which means *Jewess*) to ensnare and destroy Holofernes the commander of Nebuchadnezzar. Its purpose is to strengthen the faith of Jews who were undergoing persecution for their faith. It is not a historically accurate document; the Babylonian King Nebuchadnezzar is referred to as an Assyrian.

THE FIRST AND SECOND BOOK OF MACABEES: Contain independent accounts of events during the persecution of the Jews by Antiochus IV. Though not accepted as canonical by Jews or Protestants, these books are vital to our understanding of the history of Judaism.

THE BOOK OF WISDOM: Like Proverbs, Wisdom contains several pithy sayings and teachings. Chapter 12 beautifully explains the conquest of Canaan and chapters 13–15 deal with idolatry in a manner worthy of Isaiah. The anonymous author was an Egyptian Jew writing 100 years B.C.

THE BOOK OF SIRACH: was written in Hebrew between 200–175 B.C. by Jesus, son of Eleazar, son of Sirach. This beautiful book of wisdom literature is used extensively in Roman Catholic liturgy. In many ways it both resembles and enhances proverbs: "Wisdom's garland is fear of the Lord. With blossoms of peace and perfect health, knowledge and full understanding she showers down. She heightens the glory of those who possess her. The root of wisdom is fear of the Lord, her branches are length of days."

The writer's motive was to help his contemporaries maintain religious faith and integrity in times of trouble (ch. 2:7–10) and seems to look toward eternal judgement (ch. 7:36).

THE BOOK OF BARUCH: Is ascribed to Baruch the secretary of Jeremiah. It reports the repentance of the exiles in Babylon and claims to contain a copy of the letter Jeremiah sent to the exiles strongly condemning idolatry. Its teaching is comparable to the prophet Jeremiah's, but the book appears to be a "pious fraud."

TIMETABLE OF EVENTS

1377–1358   AKHENATON TRIES TO INTRODUCE
    MONOTHEISM TO EGYPT
1370   DAN MIGRATES NORTH
1360   BENJAMIN ALMOST WIPED OUT
1358–1349   TUTANKHAMAN'S REIGN
1316–1237   EHUD JUDGES ISRAEL
1299   HITTITES PUSH EGYPT OUT OF SYRIA
1257–1237   JABIN OPPRESSES ISRAEL
1237–1198   DEBORAH AND BARAK JUDGE ISRAEL
1198–1191   MIDIANITE OPPRESSION
1191–1151   GIDEON JUDGES ISRAEL
1069–1049   SAMSON JUDGES ISRAEL
1067–1043   SAMUEL RULES ISRAEL
1043–1011   SAUL KING
1043   SAUL SAVES JABESH-GILEAD; DEFEATS
    AMMONITES; DEFEATS PHILISTINES AT MICHMASH
1011   PHILISTINES DEFEAT SAUL AT MT. GIBOA
1011–1004   DAVID KING AT HEBRON
1005   DAVID CAPTURES JERUSALEM
1004–971   DAVID KING OVER ALL ISRAEL
971–931   SOLOMON KING OF ISRAEL
966   TEMPLE STARTED
931   KINGDOM SPLIT; REHOBOAM KING OF JUDAH
    931–913 B.C.; JEROBOAM KING OF ISRAEL 930–910 B.C.
909   BAASA KING OF ISRAEL
913–911   ABIJAM KING OF JUDAH
911–870   ASA KING OF JUDAH
885–874   OMRI KING OF ISRAEL
883–859   ASHURNASRIPAL II KING OF ASSYRIA
874–853   AHAB KING OF ISRAEL
c871   ELIJAH SLAYS THE PROPHETS OF BAAL
853   ASSYRIAN ADVANCE CHECKED AT QUARQUAR
852   ELISHA'S MINISTRY BEGINS

841   ATHALIAH MURDERS THE ROYAL PRINCES AND
       SEIZES THE THRONE OF JUDAH
835   JOASH KING OF JUDAH
796   MURDER OF ZECHARIAH
790–750   REIGN OF UZZIAH
760–745   AMOS' MINISTRY
745–715   HOSEA'S MINISTRY
715–686   REIGN OF HEZEKIAH (JUDAH)
721–705   SARGON II EMPEROR OF ASSYRIA
722   NORTHERN TRIBES TAKEN CAPTIVE
701   SENNACERIB INVADES JUDAH
640–609   JOSIAH KING OF JUDAH
626   NABOPALASSAR KING OF BABYLON
622   BOOK OF THE LAW FOUND; JOSIAH'S REFORMS
614   MEDES ATTACK ASSYRIA
612   MEDE AND BABYLONIAN FORCES DESTROY
       NINEVEH
609   JOSIAH DEFEATED BY PHARAOH NECO AT
       MEGGIDO
605   BABYLONIANS DEFEAT ASSYRIANS AND EGYP-
       TIANS AT CARCHEMISH
601   NECHO INVADES JUDAH AND JEHOIAKIM SIDES
       WITH EGYPT
597   FIRST SIEGE OF JERUSALEM
587   SECOND SIEGE OF JERUSALEM
562   DEATH OF NEBUCHADNAZZER
547   CYRUS II DEFEATS CROSEUS
539   CYRUS II OVERRUNS BABYLON
538   RETURN OF SHESHBAZZAR AND FIRST GROUP
       OF EXILES
536   TEMPLE REBUILT
520   WORK ON TEMPLE RESUMED
515   TEMPLE COMPLETED

INTRODUCTION

The New Testament details the birth, life, death, and resurrection of the Lord Jesus Christ and of the growth and persecution of the early church. It is more than a mere history, more than a theological treatise; it was written "that you may believe Jesus is the Christ and believing you may have life in his name." Jesus came "to fulfill the law and the prophets," (Mt. 5:17), "to seek and to save the lost," (Lk. 19:10), "that they may have more abundant life," (Jn. 10:10). "To all who received him, to those who believed in his name, he gave the right to become children of God," (Jn. 1:12).

In the New Testament we not only learn how to live—the sermon on the mount in Matthew 5–7 contains the greatest moral teachings ever given—but we learn how to begin eternal life now. The kingdom of God can begin in our life. It is through us as individuals, and as members of his body, the church, that God has chosen to move. We can choose to be one with Christ and God right now! Unlike the movie—Why should heaven wait?

The New Testament as we know it was written in the first century A.D. After the death of Christ, the "kerygma" or "good news" was carried by the disciples to Africa, Asia, and Europe. It was originally inseparable from the "diadche" or moral teachings of Christ. The early teachers did not have the New Testament; they had personal memories of Christ. His teachings and Old

Testament scriptures and this led to problems. In the early 40s the church almost split over the admission of Gentiles and which Jewish laws the Gentiles must observe. The Council at Jerusalem in A.D. 49 resolved the issue:

> It is my judgement, therefore, that we should not make it difficult for the Gentiles who are turning to God. Instead we should write to them, telling them to abstain from food polluted by idols, from sexual immorality, from the meat of strangled animals and from blood.
>
> Acts 15:19ff

Paul and Barnabas, together with Judas and Silas were chosen to inform the church at Antioch of this decision. Paul's letter to the Galatians gives his account of this meeting, and his letters reflect the many disputing factions in the early church. As the early disciples died or were martyred, a written code became essential and in A.D. 60 Mark wrote his gospel. The church in the 60s and 70s had only Mark's gospel and Paul's letters available.

First century Judaism and Christianity were both missionary religions. Both had moved from seeing the temple cult as the key to religious observance. The Jews of the Diaspora saw the law and its observance as most important. Christ and his followers felt that obeying God's will expressed through love, sacrifice, and faith was paramount, with Christ being the living embodiment of that will (the word became flesh). In other words, external versus internal righteousness. The Jews began to codify their written law to ensure that Jewish and Christian writings—like the Pauline epistles—were not confused. Paul's arrest and death and the persecution of the early church under Nero could have led to the church becoming insular. However, the destruction of Jerusalem in A.D. 70 brought a second Diaspora and with it came the spread of the gospel, along with heresy and conflict.

Marcion accepted Paul's epistles, stressing the love of God, but rejecting all fear. He believed in celibacy and saw procreation and the material world as evil. Luke's gospel was at one time suspect as Marcion supported it! The Montanists believed in direct communication with the Holy Spirit and rejected a formal church hierarchy. Doceitism rejected the incarnation, claiming Christ only "seemed" to become human and only "seemed" to suffer. Others were arch-conservative and tried to enforce the Torah. To establish what was "normal" Christianity, and to answer Jewish charges that the Christians in rejecting the Torah were lawless, Matthew wrote his gospel. During the persecution of Domitian, John wrote his gospel. By then the breach between the Christians and Jews had become very wide; in places he appears anti-semitic. By the end of the first century the four gospels, Paul's letters, and a book of revelation were standard in most churches. Two books of Revelation were popular: The Revelation of St. John—canonically accepted—and The Revelation of Peter.

During the systematic persecution of Christians in the second century, the wilder heresies—regarded as Christian by Rome—attracted Rome's unfavorable attention and forced the church to think out policy and seek uniformity. Origen in 203 A.D. collected Christian texts and began to determine what was canonical and what was not. Cyprian of Carthage stressed the need for discipline and obedience to the local bishop. Christianity had begun as a Jewish sect and were so regarded by Rome. They suffered when the Jews rebelled, yet the Jews regarded them as heretics and repudiated Christ. Thus the Christians had to break with the synagogue and assert the church's independence in the eyes of the Roman empire. The codification of the gospels helped. Luke's gospel is dedicated to a gentile official willing to present the Christians in a favorable light.

Both Peter and Paul were martyred in Rome, and the Roman church was the wealthiest, so the Bishop of Rome became

Primate. To guard against heresy the bishops determined what being a Christian meant and began to interpret scripture in light of the church's need. The first Roman bishop Soter 166–174 A.D. claimed his authority came from Peter (see Mt. 16:18–19), so by the third century we had Roman Catholicism. In 312 A.D. Constantine declared religious freedom for Christians in the Edict of Milan. Constantine's conversion to Christianity led to his recognition and support of the clergy. Alas, as he gave material advantages to the church he began to have a say in the running of the church. By 320 Christianity was becoming the state religion; it provided much needed welfare in an empire lacking any. Christians doctrine of hard work and obedience, together with charity and peacefulness, attracted the pagans. Ironically almost as soon as orthodox Christianity became entangled with Constantine, "The Church" began to persecute those groups who did not totally agree with them. The Catholic Church supported and taught allegiance to Rome and was a part of the state. Heresy thus became an attack on the state, and the state was happy to enforce church orthodoxy. The Donatists were the first heretics to suffer Constantine's attention. In 341 Constantine II issued the first major anti-pagan law ordering superstition eradicated. Julian the apostate, tried to turn the tide back but failed and by the end of the fourth century the Roman Empire had become "Christian" and "The Church" had become imperial.

MATTHEW

Traditionally the gospel of Matthew is attributed to the Apostle Matthew (also called Levi), a former tax collector. However, this gospel uses the gospel of Mark as a source material—it is unlikely that an eyewitness would need to do so—and was written in Greek using Greek source material during the Domitian persecution in the A.D. 90s. The attribution to Matthew may be to lend authority to the book—as Proverbs are attributed to Solomon—or it may be because the author used some of that apostle's writings. His sources include Mark, "Q" a collection of the sayings and teachings of Christ written by the apostle Matthew, and "M" material peculiar to this gospel.

Both Matthew and Luke were written during a time of crises when the church was in danger of falling apart. The Corinthian congregation deposed its bishops (Rome sent a letter known as I Clement to try and restore order), but all they had to draw on was Mark's gospel and the Pauline letters, and Marks gospel contains little teaching. To meet this need, Matthew and Luke, working independently, wrote their gospels. Both used Mark as a primary source and follow the chronology of Mark; both had access to the recorded teachings of Christ, but both also had other oral and written sources unknown to the other. Matthew's gospel is given first place in the New Testament because it ideally meets church need. It tells only stories useful for teaching and preaching, it is arranged to be easy to incorporate into church readings and organizes the teachings of Christ. It was the first gospel to be accepted as canonical in Antioch. Written primarily to show that Jesus is the Messiah of the Jews, Matthew shows that Jesus came "not to destroy the law and the prophets but to fulfill them," (Mt. 5:17).

While the Council Of Jerusalem A.D. 49 rejected strict observance of the Torah, no one reading Matthew's gospel can doubt that the Christian is called to lead a life not of slavish obedience to the written law, but to a vital living relationship with the Father that transcends, while fulfilling the law. In fact Christ shows that by over insistence on the minutia of the law, the rabbis have fallen short of God's will. "Woe to you, teachers of the law and Pharisees, you hypocrites! You give a tenth of your spices—mint, dill and cumin. But you have neglected the more important matters of the law—Justice, mercy and faithfulness," (Mt. 23:23). Uncompromisingly Christ demands our righteousness must exceed that of the scribes and pharisees; not only our deeds but our thoughts and motives must be pure!

Matthew's gospel opens with the genealogy of Jesus, drawn from a family source. He makes it clear that Jesus is the "son of David" (a messianic title), and "The son of Abraham"; (he is the Jewish Messiah). Mary, his mother, was pledged to be married to Joseph and was found "to be with child through the Holy Spirit." Joseph being a kindly man decided to put her aside quietly, but an angel appeared to him in a dream and told him the child "Jesus" will save his people from their sins. Matthew shows that this virgin birth fulfills Isaiah 7:14. Though Jesus is the savior of the Jews his appeal is universal. His genealogy includes four women, not normally counted as individuals but as a man's property and foreigners! The star proclaiming his birth was seen by Babylonian astrologers who hastened to Jerusalem seeking the great king whose star they had seen. Herod and his advisors realized the

Messiah was born and directed the Magi to Bethlehem. Herod, lacking his usual shrewdness, did not send any of his own regime with them. When the Magi were warned in a dream not to return to Herod they went home another way, while Joseph and his family fled to Egypt. Herod, in an attempt to prevent the rival king from growing up, ordered the massacre of all the boys in Bethlehem and its vicinity under two years old. Joseph, being advised in two more dreams, took his family to live in Nazareth. The gospel then leaps forward thirty years to the time of John the Baptist. John was a great man, greater than the Old Testament prophets according to Jesus (ch. 11:11). The gospels see John as the Elijah foretold in Malachi 4:5. John launched a crusade demanding repentance and social justice. Jesus' public ministry begins with his baptism by John in the Jordan. The heavens opened and he was anointed by the Holy Spirit (Messiah means anointed one). Jesus, though sinless, submitted to water baptism to consecrate himself completely to his ministry and set aside his private life and was publicly anointed by the father and the spirit. Immediately following this anointing Jesus withdrew to the desert and after fasting forty days and nights encountered Satan. The gospels stress his hunger. Research on fasting shows that after three days the body slows down and does not feel hunger again till forty days when the body, having used up all its fat tissue, begins to feed on essential tissues and acute hunger is felt. Jesus was faint and hungry. The stones littering the desert looked like little loaves. Satan , the tempter, said, "If you are the Son Of God command these stones to become bread." But Jesus answered from Deuteronomy: "Man does not live on bread alone, but on every word that comes from the mouth of God." The devil's first temptation was to misuse spiritual power to satisfy a physical need, the next was to misuse it to prove himself—to do something spectacular—and the third was to compromise. If Jesus would but worship him he would give him all the kingdoms of the world; the cross would be unnecessary. Each time Jesus rebuffed him with "the word," quoting from Deuteronomy. Jesus began his public ministry using the same basic message as John: "Repent, for the Kingdom of Heaven is near." (Compare 3:1 and 3:17.) Immediately he began to call his disciples. Unlike the great rabbis he called average working men, not to be learned theologians, but to be heralds of the kingdom seeking and saving those most in need. Jesus ministry is summed up in 4:23, teaching, preaching and healing.

Chapters 5–7 contain the essential teaching of the New Covenant. Jesus ascended the mountain, as did Moses, and proclaimed the New Torah. The Beatitudes are a challenge to the world's accepted values. They call to the deepest and best instincts in us and show how radically different God's values are from mans. Christ focuses our attention not on external observance of the law but on fulfilling God's will, of which the law is just a reflection. We not only do not murder, commit adultery or take revenge, we are called not to entertain wrath, lust or seek for vengeance. We are to love our enemies. Similarly we are not to merely give alms to be seen of men; we are to give unseen, with compassion, seeking not acclamation. Our heart must be right or the deed is worthless. The same principle applies to prayer and fasting. Jesus gives his disciples the Lord's prayer, which is not to be slavishly repeated as the heathen do (ch. 6:7). Rather in confident, loving persistence we approach God, Our Father, who knows our needs. We do not need to whine or beg. We come before him in intimacy, knowing he loves and delights in us as our Father, but also as our God. We accept that he is Sovereign Lord, that he desires our highest good and the highest good of every man. We cannot pray "thy will be done" in sincerity and go out and violate his will by exploiting or harming his other children! We humbly ask for daily bread, knowing that our father will supply our need in every realm: spiritual and emotional as well as physical. For many years I read this and saw it only as "daily bread"—my food, clothing, and shelter—but Christ was intensely aware of the spiritual reality underlying the physical, and he was a man of deep and honest emotions. He would not limit "bread" to the physical realm as the answer to our needs. He himself is the bread of life and promised that those who hunger and thirst for righteousness shall be satisfied. Christ opens the door for us to see God's sufficiency for our every need. Compare this to Psalm 23. It also reminds us that the needs we petition for must be legitimate. We pray for forgiveness and are told to forgive. Unforgiveness slams the door shut in God's face. We pray to be led not into temptation—do we deliberately flirt with temptation, exposing ourselves needlessly to enemy attack? Some of us have a problem with lust, yet read questionable material. Others have problems with drinking; nonetheless a few bottles are kept on hand, just in case company arrives. "Deliver us from evil" acknowledges our weakness and dependence on him. A man who wishes to store up treasure in heaven (ch. 6:20) has to have the guiding principle of his life straight (verse 22). He must serve God rather seeking wealth and must get free from worry. If our minds are set on God's kingdom first, our material needs will be met (ch. 6:33). He who gave us the priceless gift of life will sustain it. If we could truly grasp the teaching of Matthew 6:25–34 we would be amazed how free and untroubled our lives would become. Jesus kept his eyes on God and the troubles of this life had no power over him. In chapter 7 Jesus turns our eyes back to the power of prayer. If we ask (the Greek verb means *ask and keep on asking*), seek, and knock, God will hear us. We must trust him. We know our heavenly father will provide for our needs just as our earthly fathers would if they could. He warns us again that intimacy with God and purity of motive are more important than works and achievement (ch. 7:21–23).

Following the Sermon on the Mount are several miracles, including the raising from the dead of Jarius' daughter and the beginnings of Pharisaical opposition. In claiming to forgive sin and associating with sinners, Jesus threatened the established religious organization of the day. Jesus said, "I have come not to call the righteous but sinners." Until we realize we are sinners his message will make as little sense to us as it did to the Pharisees. Jesus' gospel is not one of comfort. It demands joyful abandonment of all but the kingdom: "Anyone who loves his father or mother more than me is not worthy of me; anyone who loves his son or daughter more than me is not worthy of me," (ch. 10:37). Nothing can stand between us and God's will for us, not even family ties. Anyone who cannot accept this will lose out on the fullness of eternal life. (Jesus provided for Mary on the cross; he does not disparage family ties. He merely demands that these legitimate duties take second place to the Kingdom.) Jesus commissions his apostles as heralds of the kingdom. The primary message is: "The kingdom of Heaven is near. Heal the sick, raise the dead, cleanse those who have leprosy. Drive out demons. Freely you have received, freely give," (ch. 10:7). Jesus healing on the Sabbath intensifies the opposition of religious leaders and they began to plot his death (ch. 13:14).

Jesus' cousin John was beheaded by Herod in chapter 14. Filled with sorrow he withdrew to a solitary place, but found a large crowd had followed him. Jesus "had compassion on them and healed their sick." This is a vague reflection of the cross. In deep distress, needing privacy to mourn, Jesus set aside his own legitimate need and moved with compassion, ministering to the crowds. He attended not only to their spiritual and physical healing and needs but to their hunger as well. Following the calming of the storm and the healings at Gennesaret, Jesus again encountered the Pharisees and teachers who were shocked to see Jesus' disciples failing to observe ritual purity laws. Jesus took the opportunity to show the difference between ritual and heart purity. Motives are more important than trappings and observances. He cited the Pharisees' use of tradition to avoid helping aged parents. Men using tradition to avoid obeying the moral law sickened and angered him. Following this sharp conflict Jesus withdrew to Tyre and Sidon; there a Canaanite woman asked him to heal her daughter. This passage of scripture is confusing. Jesus appears at first unwilling to help her. His disciples ignore her need; she is just a nuisance. "Send her away, for she keeps crying after us." Jesus says, "It is not right to take the children's bread and toss it to their dogs." Scholars argue about the exact meaning of Jesus' word "dogs," whether Jesus was testing the woman's faith or rebuking his disciples for their hardness of heart. The woman was certainly not deterred by the apparent coldness of his words; she knew Jesus could heal her daughter and was confident that he would. The Jewish leaders (the children) have rejected the bread of life (Jesus), and the dogs (Gentiles) are eager for it. She asks for whatever crumbs of mercy he will give. Jesus heals her child. In chapter 16 Jesus, after further conflict with the Pharisees, challenges his disciples, "What about you? Who do you say I am?" Peter replies, "You are the Christ, the Son of the Living God." In turn Jesus replies, "You are Peter, and on this rock I will build my church," a verse often quoted by The Roman Catholic Church to support the primacy of the Roman bishop. Other scholars argue that the "rock" was Peter's declaration: "You are the Christ, the Son of the Living God." This truth is the bedrock or foundation of our faith. Almost immediately after this declaration Jesus predicts his death, and in horror Peter cries, "Never, Lord! This shall never happen to you," and is rebuked. "Get behind me Satan! You are a stumbling block to me; you do not have in mind the things of God, but the things of men." Even in love, we cannot spare others from "the cross"—God's will for them.

Jesus' singleness of vision in chapter 18 is totally uncompromising. "If your eye causes you to sin, gouge it out and throw it away. It is better for you to enter life with one eye than to have two eyes and be thrown into the fire of hell." Better the most cruel self-denial than the loss of true life and a relationship with God. Jesus' command to the rich young ruler in chapter 19 is in a similar vein. If riches or a desire for them corrupt our morals, get rid of them! Jesus did not sweepingly condemn all rich men; Zacchaeus, Nicodemus, Lazarus, Joseph of Arimathea and the host for the last supper were rich. But keeping riches and integrity is hard—almost impossible—and only God's grace makes it possible. Jesus triumphal entry into Jerusalem intensifies his struggle with the Jewish leaders. In Chapter 22 the Pharisees, Herodians and Sadducees unite against Jesus. Jesus adroitly answers the most difficult questions posed: Should we pay tax to Caesar (the Roman Emperor) or not? Yes, render to Caesar what is Caesar's and to God what is God's. Yes, the resurrection is real. The greatest commandment is "Love the Lord your God with all your heart and with all your soul and with all your mind. The second is like it, love your neighbor as yourself." These two commandments sum up the whole law and the prophets. Chapter 23 warns against the leaders who try to add to these commandments for their own self-exaltation. Chapter 24 warns of the fall of Jerusalem (fulfilled in A.D. 70) and tells us how we will know the last days. Chapter 25:31–46 picture the Last Judgement. God judges men not on religious observance but on social and moral grounds. Did you feed the hungry? Show hospitality to the stranger and homeless? Did you have compassion; did you meet the needy at the point of their need? The result of this parable is "the chief priests and the elders of the people assembled . . . and they plotted to arrest Jesus in some sly way and kill him." Judas, one of the twelve, joined the conspiracy. Matthew is not interested in Judas' motive. John says it was greed. Luke says, "Satan entered into him." Scholars argue over what motivated him. Taylor Caldwell's novel *I, Judas* supports the popular view that Judas betrayed Christ to force him to reveal himself and lead the revolt against Rome.

At the moving ceremony of the Last Supper, Jesus plainly told the disciples he would be betrayed and die. After the breaking of the bread and sharing the wine, they sang a hymn and went to the Mount of Olives. Jesus predicted Peters denial of him, but Peter and the others indignantly replied, "Even if I have to die with you, I will never disown you." In the garden of Gethsemane Christ was "overwhelmed with sorrow." He fell face down on the ground and prayed, "My father, if it is possible may this be taken from me. Yet not as I will but as you will." Some ministers believe that Christ saved us in Gethsemane, that the spiritual battle took place in this lonely garden, while his friends slept. In Gethsemane Christ stood alone, misunderstood. He saw the flood of wickedness that was to flood over him, the scapegoat for our sin. His word and work seemed eclipsed in failure and a cruel and painful death beckoned. There he surrendered his will to God. "Not as I will but as thou wilt." Once he knew the cross was God's will, there was no other way. His will and self-life being crucified already, he arose and went to his death. He would not suffer his companions to fight the temple guard. "Then all the disciples left him and fled."

Jesus was led before the Sanhedrin for a rigged trial. The meeting was not held at the stated place, nor in daytime, nor was the charge of blasphemy sustained by the evidence. Caiaphas solemnly charged Jesus under oath to answer if he was the Christ. Jesus replied, "Yes, it is as you say." Caiaphas tore his clothes and accused Christ of blasphemy. They condemned him to death. Peter had followed him. But still in the grip of fear, Peter denied Christ when challenged in the forecourt. In the morning they led Jesus before Pilate. Judas, filled with remorse, tried to give back the thirty pieces of silver and finding he was too late hanged himself.

When Jesus was brought before Pilate he was tried, not for blasphemy, but for treason against the Roman Empire. Pilate knew the charge to be false. He tried to free Jesus "for he knew that for envy they had delivered him." Pilate offered to free Jesus or an insurrectionist known as Barabbas. The word play is interesting; Pilate asked the Jews: Will I release Barabbas—the name means *son of the father*—or Jesus the Christ, the anointed one. The Jews choose Barabbas and agreed that as for Christ, "His blood be upon us and upon our children." Only Matthew records Pilate's wife sending a warning to her husband. "Have thou nothing to do with that just man: For I have suffered many things this day in a dream because of him" (the Greek church canonized Claudia Procla for this). After the scourging, the soldiers mocked Jesus. They put a scarlet robe and crown of thorns on him and mockingly bowed, crying, "Hail the king of the Jews." They came to Golgotha and crucified him. It was Roman custom to put a titulus around the neck of a criminal stating the crime for which he was condemned. The crime for which Jesus was executed was "This is Jesus the king of the Jews." On the cross, the crowds, chief priests, elders and fellow dying prisoners mocked him. After six hours of agony, three of which were during supernatural darkness, Jesus cried, "Eli, Eli, Lama Sabachtani"—My God, My God, why have you forsaken me? Psalm 22, here quoted was a prayer of complaint which ended in triumph and which pious Jews used in terms of adversity. Jesus cried again and died. The veil of the temple was torn. The lintel on which the curtain separating the holiest of holies from the holy place hung shattered of itself on the day Jesus died. The temple leaders had betrayed the covenant and God showed his displeasure. Only Matthew records the opening of the graves. The centurion and the soldiers with him, seeing this were afraid and said, "Truly this was the son of God." Joseph of Arimathae buried Jesus. The chief priests and Pharisees begged Pilate to guard the tomb. He agreed.

Following the sabbath the women went to the tomb and there saw an angel who told them, "Go quickly, tell his disciples that he is risen from the dead." As they went they met Jesus, who like the angel, told them that he would meet his brethren in Galilee. The soldiers reported to the high priests, who bribed them to say that the disciples stole the body. The disciples met Jesus at a mountain in Galilee. There they worshiped him, not just as friend and teacher but as Risen Lord and Messiah. There they received the Great Commission: "Go, therefore, and make disciples of all nations, baptizing them in the name of the Father and of the Son and of the Holy Spirit, teaching them to observe all that I have commanded you; and lo, I am with you always, to the close of the age."

MARK

Mark's gospel was the earliest gospel to be written c62 A.D. Both Matthew and Luke use Mark as a source document and keep to the same chronology. Mark's gospel was written during the persecution of the church by Nero. Its aim was to set forth the message of salvation through Jesus Christ as proclaimed by the apostolic church. Mark is not writing a defense of Christianity or to win converts; he is writing to encourage believers whose Christianity may very well mean physical death. When Mark writes, "Whoever wants to save his life will lose it, but whoever loses his life for me and the gospel will save it" (Mk. 9:35), he means it—literally! His gospel is a call to courage and stresses the heroic ethics demanded with Christ as a supreme example. John the Baptist fearlessly denouncing Herod's immorality is a second. This gospel contains little teaching; it was not intended to be a theological training document or to promote a specific doctrine. Jesus' Passion is the central theme.

Authorship of this gospel is usually attributed to John Mark, Paul's fickle companion and Peter's interpreter. Mark's gospel was based upon oral tradition, with which he dealt very faithfully. Papias, Bishop of Hierapolis in A.D. 140 wrote, "Mark committed no error in writing certain matters just as he remembered them. For he had only one object in view, namely to leave out nothing of the things which he had heard and to include no false statement among them."

Mark opens abruptly: "The beginning of the gospel about Jesus Christ, the Son of God," and launches without further pre-amble into the appearance of John the Baptist. Jesus' baptism and the temptations are mentioned but not elaborated upon. After the call of the first four disciples, Jesus casts out a demon on the Sabbath. Casting out demons was believed to be a messianic privi-lege. This together with several healings drew him to the atten-tion of the religious leaders of the day. Jesus did not fit the tradi-tional messiah role, here was no warrior king descended directly from David! His claim to forgive sins shocked the Pharisees. "Why does this fellow talk like that? He's blaspheming! Who can forgive sins but God alone." The fact that he could match words with deeds was yet more alarming.

Chapter 2 contains four episodes of conflict with the Pharisees:

(1) Why does this fellow talk like this?

(2) Why does he eat with tax collectors and sinners?

(3) How is it that John's disciples and the disciples of the Pharisees fast often but yours do not?

(4) Why are they doing what is unlawful to do on the Sabbath?

In each case Jesus appealed to the greater truth. The paralyt-ic's obvious need was physical healing, but he desperately need spiritual solace. Jesus came to call sinners (not righteous) to repentance. The disciples broke no mosaic law by plucking ears of grain on a Sabbath, yet David did break the law in a case of extremity. In chapter 3 Jesus once more heals on the Sabbath and asks, "Which is lawful to do on the Sabbath: to do good or to do evil, to save life or to kill it?" Though this gospel does not contain the great body of sayings common to Matthew and Luke, it is obvious that Jesus looks beyond the law to the spiritual issues involved. He rejects external-only religion vehemently (Mk. 7:14–15). The widows mite is of greater worth to Jesus than all the wealth of the Pharisees. The only kind of faith worth having is faith willing to renounce all worldly wealth (ch. 10:21), all personal desires and ambitions (verse 42), social standing and family ties if they hinder wholehearted devotion to the kingdom and its extension. Rather than proving his messiahship to the the religious leaders, Jesus' continuous exorcisms drew their accusation. "He is possessed by Beelzebub!" "By the prince of demons he is driving out demons." They refuse to accept him because he does not fit their preconceived ideas about what the messiah will be like. Jesus answers this charge twice: Satan would not fight himself, or his kingdom would fall. Moreover there were several Jewish exorcists. Were they also possessed? He issues one of the direst warnings given in scripture, "Whoever blasphemes against the Holy Spirit will never be forgiven; he is guilty of an eternal sin," (Mk. 3:29). Men may blaspheme Christ through ignorance; blasphemy against the Holy Spirit is to call good evil and evil good. It is a distortion of the whole spiritual being so that we become incapable of recognizing good. It is evidence of moral perverseness. Some theologians say that the blasphemer is incapable of repentance.

Jesus' exorcism in the region of Geraseneses provokes a similar reaction. His power is feared more than the semi-controllable demoniac and he is begged to depart. In chapter 5 Jesus raises a dead girl to life, and heals a woman with a hemorrhage. Evidence of Mark's straightforwardness is seen in verse 31. Jesus, sensitive to the needs of one individual asks, "Who touched me?" The disciples answer abruptly, "Thou seest the multitude thronging thee, and sayest thou, who touched me?' This passage is modified in Luke. Both Jesus' question and the response are omitted in Matthew. Mark sees no need to hide the disciples failings. They were men. In Nazareth Jesus found cynical disbelief and was "amazed" but undaunted and sent the apostles out to preach. Herod, hearing of Jesus, was filled with superstitious dread, having murdered John to please his step-daughter. The monarch feared Jesus was John risen from the dead.

Jesus retired to a solitary place but found the crowd awaiting him. Filled with compassion he taught them and fed 5,000 men with five loaves and two fishes. Departing to Gennaseret he was again besieged by multitudes. Chapter 7 records another sharp conflict with the Pharisees. Jesus' disciples did not observe the ritual purity laws. Jesus rebuked the pharisees, "You have let go the commands of God and are holding on to the traditions of men." He insists that

> nothing that enters a man from the outside can make him unclean. For it does not go into his heart but into his stomach (verse 18). What comes out of a man is what makes him unclean. For from within, out of men's hearts, come evil thoughts, sexual immorality, theft, murder, adultery, greed, malice, deceit, lewdness, envy, slander, arrogance and folly. All these evils come from inside and make a man unclean.

Mark begins to move surely toward the passion with Jesus' three predictions of his death: chapter 8:31, 9:31 and 10:33. His disciples remain obtuse. Peter rebukes him on the first occasion; on the second his disciples are busy arguing which of them is the greatest; and on the third James and John ask to sit at his right and left hand when he takes his throne. The disciples, even at this late date, are still expecting a military messiah. The transfiguration moves Peter, to want to build booths! Coming down from the mountain Jesus found a large crowd arguing with the other nine disciples who were unable to exorcise a boy possessed with a dumb demon. The boy's father begged, "If you can do anything take pity on us and help us." Jesus asked, "If you can? Everything is possible for him who believes." The fathers reply is one that finds an echo in most men's aching hearts: "I do believe; help me overcome my unbelief." Jesus exorcised the child and for the second time predicted his own death.

In chapter 10 Jesus insists that we accept the kingdom as a little child, humbly and without self-righteousness. We should receive joyfully and gladly without feelings of pride. And we must never try to buy our way in as the Jewish religious leaders and Catholics at the time of the reformation were. The rich young ruler is ordered to sell all, give all, and follow Jesus. His walking away with great sorrow illustrates how often our possessions own us, not the reverse. The passage ends with words of solace to the persecuted church. "No one who has left home or brothers or sisters or mother or father or children or fields for me and the gospel will fail to receive a hundred times as much in this present age (homes, brothers, sisters, mothers, children and fields—and with them persecutions—and in the age to come eternal life (ch. 10:29–30). This is followed immediately by Jesus' third prediction of his own death. He does not ask us to face anything he has not already faced. Jesus entered Jerusalem in triumph on Palm Sunday, amid crowds crying, "Hosannah Blessed is he who comes in the name of the Lord." Less than a week later, he would die with mobs howling, "Crucify him."

Jesus began the last week of his life driving out the traders in the temple. These men were in the outer court and had legitimate business being there under Jewish law. Jesus was filled with zeal for his father's house and could not bear to see the temple of God used as a market. Only Mark has the phrase "and (he) would not allow anyone to carry merchandise through the temple courts," but all the gospels describe this incident. This action, perhaps more than his teaching, incited the chief priests and teachers of the law to begin "looking for a way to kill him, for they feared him." He was overturning their world and threatening their livlihood. Angrily they demanded, "By what authority are you doing these things?" believing Jesus had no legal or spiritual right to act as he did. The answer Jesus gave, by inference from his question about John was, "from God." The parable following, the tenants in the vineyard, is a lament for the wickedness and hardness of their hearts and a prediction of his own death. Angry and fearful but more determined than ever they departed. The Herodians joined in the plot trying to trick Jesus into speaking against Rome. The Sadducees also arrived with trick questions. At last all the Jewish political and religious leaders were in agreement; Christ must die! The question of whether or not he was the messiah was not pertinent; he threatened their wallet! Jesus prediction of the destruction of the temple in A.D. 70 was to be misinterpreted and used against him at his trial. In chapter 13 Jesus prophecies both the destruction of Jerusalem and the end of the world. Reading this chapter requires great caution. Jesus clearly tells us, however, that we are not to waste time calculating the exact date of the end for "no one knows about that day or hour not even the angels in heaven, nor the son, but only the father. Be on guard! Be alert! You do not know when that time will come," (Mk. 13:32–33). At Bethany, Mary of Magdala anointed Jesus with "an alabaster jar of very expensive perfume, made from pure nard. She broke the jar and poured the perfume on his head." Many were indignant at this waste of a year's wages! But Jesus exulted in her act. She recklessly gave the most precious possession she had and poured out her all in sorrowing repentance for her sin (traditionally she was a harlot). Jesus again predicted his death: "She poured perfume on my body beforehand to prepare for my burial." There is no indication in Mark's gospel that anyone other than the weeping Mary comprehended or cared about his words.

Judas Iscariot went to the chief priests and agreed to help them capture Jesus. The account of the last supper in Mark has a solemn dignity about it. "One of you will betray me—one who is eating with me." Saddened they all began to ask, "Surely not I?" Jesus warned them that they would all fall away, but Peter boldly proclaimed that he would not, "Even if I have to die with you, I will never disown you." Arriving at Gethsemane Jesus asked eight of the disciples to "sit here while I pray." Peter, James and John he took further into the garden, telling them his soul was overwhelmed with sorrow and asked them to keep watch. Though the disciples fell asleep and left him to face the agony of that hour alone, the father did not suffer the traitor and soldiers to come till Jesus finished his prayer and all doubt and fear were conquered. "Abba, father, everything is possible for you. Take this cup from me, yet not what I will but what you will." As Jesus rejoined the disciples, Judas arrived with the crowd sent by the chief priests and arrested him. Only Mark's gospel notes the anonymous disciple who tried to follow but when seized fled leaving his garment behind. Some speculate that Mark, himself, was the nameless youth.

At Jesus' trial the witnesses could not agree. His teaching on the resurrection was misquoted and misinterpreted as desiring the destruction of the temple. When Jesus acknowledged his messiahship the Sanhedrin decided he was guilty of blasphemy and condemned him to die. Outside Peter denied him as the rooster began to crow. The Sanhedrin could not condemn a man to death, so Jesus was brought before Pilate. Pilate knew Jesus was innocent and had been handed over "out of envy." He tried to free him, but wanting to appease the mob who were howling "crucify him," he had Jesus flogged and handed him over to be crucified. It took Jesus six hours to die. From a distance, Mary of Magdala, his mother and many other women watched. Joseph of Arimathea bravely asked Pilate for the body and buried him. Very early on the first day of the week, the women went to the tomb and found the stone rolled away. Inside a young man, dressed in a white robe told them, "He has risen." Showing Christ's deep love and compassion the angel continued, "Tell his disciples, and Peter, he is going ahead of you into Galilee. There you will see him, just as he told you." The women fled. At this point the gospel of Mark originally ended. Perhaps the last page was lost, or perhaps Mark ended as abruptly as he began. The longer ending, verses 9–20, is based on other gospel passages and the beginning of acts and may have been added by an editor in the second century. A tenth century Armenian manuscript attributes it to Ariston, a presbyter.

LUKE

It is generally accepted that both the Gospel of Luke and the Book of Acts were written by the same author. Most probably St. Luke, the "dear and glorious physician" who was Paul's companion and friend. Irenaus in A.D. 185 ascribed both books to Luke. Both volumes were in use by A.D. 110 and were written during the reign of Domitian (81–96 A.D.). Luke's gospel is the most beautiful book of the New Testament in many ways. Luke and Deutro-Isaiah have the same vision of Christ: the suffering servant sent to redeem mankind. In Luke's gospel, John the Baptist proclaims, "All mankind will see God's salvation," and only Luke records Simeon's prophecy that the Christ will be "a light for revelation to the gentiles and for glory to your people Israel," (Lk. 2:32). When Jesus first preached at Nazareth he declared, quoting from Isaiah,

> The spirit of the Lord is on me, because he has anointed me to preach the good news to the poor. He has sent me to proclaim freedom for the prisoners and recovery of sight for the blind, to release the oppressed, to proclaim the year of the Lord's favor.

He then reminded his hearers that both Elijah and Elisha ministered among the heathen. Salvation will not be limited to the

Jewish nation. Luke was intensely aware of Christ's mission, "To seek and to save the lost." No one reading his gospel can doubt that Christ is the savior of all mankind. Jesus reaches out to the poor, to the sinners, the despised tax-collectors and to the Roman centurion. He respects women, and they are among the most faithful of his followers. He is filled with compassion, a compassion that recognizes no boundaries either of race or class. Jesus demands genuine repentance and is more than willing to embrace the repentant Zaccheus while religious leaders who trust in their own righteousness face his scorn. (See the parable of the Pharisee and the tax-collector, Luke 18:9–14.)

Luke's nativity stories came from a source unknown to the other synoptics. He stresses the miraculous nature of John's birth, a detail omitted by the other evangelists, and links John and Jesus inseparably. John is the messenger foretold in Malachi. Even in the womb John leaps for joy at Christ's presence. Luke lay great emphasis on Mary's virginity. Christ was not just a great prophet; he was the Son of God. Pagan nations have many stories of the sons of gods, but the birth of Christ has no such connotations. Mary is young, pure, and rather frightened at the angels appearance. When she is told she will bear a son she asks how? The angel answers, "The Holy Spirit will come upon you and the power of the most high will overshadow you. So the holy one to be born will be called the Son of God." Luke records Mary's beautiful song, The Magnificat, and Zachariah's song on the birth of John. Both these beautiful poems are revolutionary. Mary rejoices in her exaltation and God's mercy but also that

He has scattered those who are proud in their inmost thoughts. He has brought down rulers from their thrones but has lifted up the humble. He has filled the hungry with good things but has sent the rich empty away.

143

In the beatitudes Jesus echoes her sentiment, "Blessed are you who are poor for yours is the kingdom of heaven . . . Woe to you who are rich for you have already received your reward." Luke sees worldly prosperity as a snare preventing men from seeking the kingdom of God. John's call for repentance is primarily concerned with repentance regarding money. The man with two coats must share, likewise the man with food. The tax-collectors are told, "Don't collect any more than you are required to"; the soldiers, "Don't exhort money and don't accuse anyone falsely. Be content with your pay." It is riches that prevent the rich young ruler from following Christ and love of money that causes the Pharisees to reject him. Zachaeus repents and gives away half his fortune and is willing to repay fourfold anyone he defrauded. While money is not inherently evil, possession of it makes entry into the kingdom almost impossible. Men who are rich in this world do not seek the riches of heaven. Those who are well fed are unaware of their spiritual hunger. Luke's beatitudes are more primitive than Matthew's and more revolutionary! His woes strike directly at our purse and belly. Are we comfortable and at home in this world? Then woe to us, we will lose out on the Kingdom. Luke's parable of the rich fool forcibly drives home his point. "A man's life does not consist in the abundance of his possessions," (ch. 12:15). We must not store up things; we must be rich toward God.

> Do not set your heart on what you will eat or drink; do not worry about it. For the pagan world runs after all such things, and your father knows that you need them. But seek his kingdom and these things will be given to you as well.

We are urged to "provide purses for yourselves that will not wear out, a treasure in heaven that will not be exhausted, where no thief comes near and no moth destroys. For where your treasure is, there your heart will be also." Both Luke's gospel and the book of Acts stress our responsibility to be proper stewards of money, hoarding it will lead to spiritual death. "You cannot serve both God and money," (Lk. 16:13). In the parable of the rich man and Lazarus, the rich man is condemned not for being rich but for ignoring the needs of the beggar who sat on his own doorstep. His condemnation is for hardness of heart as well as for misuse of wealth.

Luke also lays great emphasis on the work of the Holy Spirit. The spirit is mentioned seventeen times in this gospel (fifty-seven times in Acts) but only six times in Mark and twelve times in Matthew. Emphasis is also given to prayer. In Luke's gospel Jesus is continually in prayer. Before every major decision Jesus prays, and his last words are a prayer, "Father into thy hands I commit my spirit." The parable of the widow and the unjust judge stresses our need for perseverance in prayer. Even Jesus had to pray the same urgent prayer three times in Gethsemane! We must not be weary in prayer. It is not primarily to bend God to our will, but for us to enter his presence and get to know him. Through prayer we are drawn into unity with Christ and God. It is prayer which conveys God's will to earth.

Like Mark, Luke demands singleness of vision and purpose. Anything that comes between us and the kingdom must be removed. Luke stresses that Jesus was crucified due to the animosity of the Jews, not through Pilate's desire. He is at pains to show Theophilus that though Jesus was executed as a revolutionary, "The King of the Jews," Christianity was not a subversive sect. Jesus commanded, "Give to Caesar what is Caesar's, and to God what is God's." His kingdom was not of this world. Jesus even healed the servant of the high priest who was sent to arrest him (ch. 22:51). Both Herod and Pilate found Christ innocent of any crime. Pilate three times tried to free Christ before yielding to the demands of the mob to crucify him. This gospel closes with the

Ascension and the disciples returning to Jerusalem to await the arrival of the Holy Spirit. "And they stayed continually at the temple praising God." It is at this point that Luke's second book Acts opens.

JOHN

Tradition ascribes the fourth gospel to John, son of Zebedee, the beloved disciple. Some theologians believe that the gospel was written not by the apostle John, but by a disciple of his using John's memoirs. Also that it was written in Ephesus toward the close of the first century, after the formal break with the synagogue. This gospel is written "that you may believe that Jesus is the Christ, the son of God and that believing you may have life in his name." There is no "messianic secret" in John's gospel. Jesus refers to "he who sent me" twenty-six times and stresses that he is one with the father (the Jews try to stone him for this declaration). John's gospel was written at a time when heresy was rampant. Docetism taught that matter was inherently evil and denied the incarnation. To this John boldly states, "The Word became flesh." John's gospel shows a more human Jesus than the synoptics. Jesus gets tired, thirsty, he weeps with compassion, he offers Thomas his wounded hands to touch. He is *real*. Yet John never for a moment lets us think that Jesus is but a man. He is the Son of God. The whole gospel is filled with a exultant and triumphant certainty that Jesus is the logos, the Word of God, sent by the Father to bring men to the truth. He is the light of the world, the bread of life, living water, the resurrection and the life. Jesus is man. As a man we can walk with him, eat with him, laugh with him and weep with him, be one with him. But he is God, the perfect revelation of the Father. He does nothing of his own will and lives to fulfill the father's purpose. Through him we can be one with the Father! Jesus prays,

> I am not praying for the world but for those whom thou hast given me, for they are thine, all mine are thine, and thine are mine, and I am glorified in them. And now I am no more in the world, but they are in the world, and I am coming to thee. Holy Father, keep them in thy name which thou hast given me, that they may be one, even as we are one.

In chapter 14 he promises, "If anyone loves me, he will obey my teaching, my father will love him and we will come to him and make our home with him." The synoptic gospels try to give the history of Jesus' ministry. John does so too, but his primary concern is not to write a biography but to convey the truth that Jesus is Lord, true man and true God, and through belief in him we have salvation (Jn. 3:18–20), and rebirth into the kingdom (ch. 3:16). In fact "to all who received him, to those who believed in his name, he gave the right to become children of God." John's gospel is not so much a catechism or history, rather, it is a theological message grounded in historical fact, and only those facts are given which promote the thrust of the book "that you may believe." The last verse in the gospel tells us bluntly that this book is not, nor was it intended to be a record of all Jesus did and said. John omits many important historical moments and concentrates on revealing Jesus. A secondary strand of this glorious revelation is that union with God in Christ, though demanding self-renunciation, is not some absorption into the deity or "nirvana" (blessed nothingness). It is "life, more abundant life." It allows us fellowship with God, and this fellowship is conditioned by obedience to love! We obey Christ because we love him; we love our brothers because he so commanded, and because it is impossible to serve him who is all love and compassion without loving each other. Every obstacle to love is crushed by Christ. He allows us no room for selfishness—which brings death—or pride, or unforgiveness.

The gospel opens with a dramatic and beautiful poem:

> In the beginning was the Word, and the Word was with God and the Word was God. The same was in the beginning with God. All things were made by him and without him was not anything made that was made. In him was life and the life was the light of men.

The whole truth of the gospel account is here summed up. Jesus was God, eternally coexistent with the Father. He was creator; he is life and light.

This gospel refers more to John the Baptist than the other gospels, (though it omits Salome's dance). John is the messenger, the friend of the bridegroom. He joyfully sends his disciples after Christ, the light of the world, and bears witness to him, even when he begins to lose his own following and his imprisonment and death draw near. Jesus' first miracle in this gospel (which is not recorded in the other gospels) at the wedding feast of Canaan shows a gentle and fun loving side of Christ. He is welcomed at festivals. His presence brings joy! He is no stern visaged puritan condemning all fun. He enjoys the innocent pleasures of life and saves his friends from embarrassment.

Chapter 3 is the most quoted chapter in the Bible. Nicodemus, a Pharisee and member of the Sanhedrin, came to Jesus in private to question him. Jesus told him, "No one can see the Kingdom of God unless he is born again." The Aramaic means "born from above"—from God. Jesus demands not reform but renewal. If the new life is to be lived there must be a new creature, wholly new. God can make us totally new, with a heart filled with compassion like Christ's, shrinking from evil and moving in harmony with God's slightest touch. We can be "sons of God." God's motive in sending Christ was to make this possible. If we accept Christ, we can begin to live this eternal life, but "whoever does not believe stands condemned already because he has not believed in the name of God's one and only son." Jesus pulls no punches: if you love God, if you love the truth you will come to him; if you reject him you do so because you do evil and fear exposure (ch. 3:20). Chapters 1:19 through 20:31 are the enacted drama of the light (Christ) versus the darkness. Unfortunately it is those who appear to be righteous who have justified themselves by their actions who refuse the light. They cannot accept that they too are sinners and fall short of God's requirements. They are so much better than their fellow man! Jesus is condemned by the self-righteous for Sabbath-breaking and fellowship with sinners, for failure to meet the strict demands of the ceremonial law.

The universal nature of Christ's mission is shown much earlier in John's gospel than in the synoptic accounts. Jesus leaving Jerusalem to return to Galilee has to pass through Samaria. There tired and thirsty he rests at a well and encounters a sinful Samaritan woman and tells her he is the living water, the messiah. He stayed, a welcome guest for two days, and "many more became believers." Arriving in Galilee he heals the royal official's son. Some time later he returned to Jerusalem, once again to encounter hostility for healing on the Sabbath. His defense—"my father is always at his work to this very day, and I, too am working"—stirs the Jews to try harder to kill him. In chapter 6 Jesus feeds the 5,000, miraculously multiplying five loaves and two fish to feed the great crowd following him. Sadly this results in the crowd deciding to make Jesus king by force, against his will, so quietly he withdrew alone to the mountain. He was followed across the lake by the crowd, not because they desired salvation or to hear him, but because he fed them. Jesus' cry then, as it is today is, "Do not work for food that spoils but for food that endures to eternal life. . . . The bread of God is he who comes down from heaven and gives life to the world." Jesus tells the disciples to "eat this bread," to absorb his teaching, his character, his mind, his ways. We must appropriate (eat) all of him! A turning point is reached. Those who wanted merely a material kingdom and material benefits left him (ch. 6:66). Jesus asked the twelve, "You do not want to leave too, do you?" Peter, as spokesman, replied "Lord, to whom shall we go? You have the words of eternal life. We believe and know that you are the Holy One of God." Jesus' family were as confused as the multitudes (ch. 7:5). At the Feast of the Tabernacles, Jesus plainly announced that he was "the living water," the source of life, and the crowds were divided. He promised, "If you hold to my teaching you are really my disciples. Then you will know the truth and the truth will set you free." Indignantly the crowd replied, we have never been slaves! Jesus spoke of a different kind of freedom: freedom from sin; freedom from fear and greed, hatred, selfishness and materialism; freedom to live as a whole man and have fellowship with God. Angrily the Jews accused him of being a Samaritan and being demon possessed. Jesus further proclaimed that "if anyone keeps my word, he will never see death." This led the Jews to try and stone him.

Jesus' healing of the blind man, again on the Sabbath, added fuel to the fires of opposition. This time the healing also led to persecution of the person touched by Jesus. The man's refusal to deny Christ led to his being thrown out of the synagogue, as many early Christians were to be. Instead of convincing the leaders that he is the resurrection and the life, Jesus' raising of Lazarus from the dead hardened their hearts further, and they decided to kill both Lazarus and Christ. The attitude of the Jewish leaders horrifies us. They did not care whether or not Jesus was the messiah; they only wanted to maintain the status quo (ch. 11:47–48). The second half of John's gospel describes "the passion." Jesus entered Jerusalem in triumph (ch. 12:12–19) and immediately predicted his death, but promises that this death will "produce many seeds." This brief passage is the ultimate warning against selfishness. "Unless a kernel of wheat falls to the ground and dies it remains only a single seed. But if it dies, it produces many seeds. The man who loves his life will lose it, while the man who hates his life in this world will keep it for eternal life." This seeming paradox points us to the way of life. If we live for ourselves alone, our life becomes meaningless and drab. Those who give freely, without counting the cost, like Christ live the abundant life and inspire others to follow them.

Chapter 13, the account of washing the disciples feet, is unique to John. The custom in Palestine was that in wealthy households a slave would wash the travel-stained feet of the guests. In poorer houses one of the guests, or the host would. The disciples were unwilling to humble themselves to preform this menial task. Having arrived in Jerusalem, they knew the kingdom would soon be revealed. In Mark's account James and John had already requested to sit at the right and left hand of Christ. The other disciples were angry with them. Perhaps the meal was passed in cold silence. Christ could not endure it! He, the master, took off his outer clothing and began to wash the feet of his disciples. Peter horrified tried to stop him. Gently Jesus rebuked his sullen followers, "Now that I, your Lord and teacher have washed your feet, you also should wash one another's feet. I have set you an example that you should do as I have done for you." In Mark, Jesus gently reminded them, "the Son of Man came not to be served but to be serve." Jesus turns our priorities upside down. Pride, self righteousness and self justification lead to hardness of heart which precludes repentance. While awareness of our sin, of our own unworthiness, leads to repentance and a humbled heart. This allows the grace, the light of God to flow through us unhindered. Jesus warned the disciples that one of their number is the traitor who will betray him. Judas slunk out, while Peter protested, "I will lay down my life for you." Sadly Jesus warned Peter that he will deny him three times before the cock crows. Chapters 14–16 teach the disciples they must rely on Christ as their root. Their life is to be with him, and that means to be one with the father. Chapter 17 records Christ's prayer for himself, for the apostles, and for the church. As he finished praying, Judas arrived with "soldiers and some officials from the chief priests and Pharisees." Peter tried to defend him but Jesus rebuked him, "Put your sword away! Shall I not drink the cup the father has given me?" He was arrested and brought before Annais and Caiphas. Unable to impose the death sentence they sent him to Pilate. Pilate has earned contempt and hatred for generations because he ordered the execution of Christ, yet Pilate was an unwilling participant in the passion narrative. He at first told the Jews, "Take him yourselves and judge him by your own law." When they said they did not have the right to execute anyone, Pilate talked briefly with Christ and a second time appealed to the crowd. Jesus was scourged and crowned with thorns, and a third time Pilate appealed to the crowd who demanded, "Crucify! Crucify!" The gospel records, "Pilate tried to set Jesus free, but the Jews kept shouting, "If you let this man go, you are no friend of Caesar. Anyone who claims to be a king opposes Caesar." Pilate could not risk the wrath of Tiberias. Finally he gave in, but yet took a slight revenge on the Jews. The crime for which Jesus was crucified was that of being "the King of the Jews." The leaders protested. Earlier they had cried, "we have no king but Caesar." Now they balk, "Do not write 'the King of the Jews,' but that this man *claimed* to be the king of the Jews." Pilate answered, "What I have written I have written." Jesus was crucified at Golgotha. His mother, aunt,

Mary the wife of Clopas and Mary Magdalene stood at the cross with John. Jesus told John to care for his mother, and after saying, "It is finished," died.

Joseph of Arimathea asked Pilate for his body, and with Nicodemus prepared Christ for burial. Mary Magdalene went to the tomb on the day after the sabbath and saw the stone rolled away. She ran to Peter and John fearfully crying, "They have taken the Lord out of the tomb and we don't know where they have put him!" Peter and John ran to the tomb, "saw and believed." Mary had returned to the tomb. She sought Jesus and would not leave without seeing her Lord. And she was the first to see him, clad only in a loincloth, and to talk to him. Once again she was the messenger, this time with a positive and glorious message, "I have seen the Lord." That evening he appeared to the disciples and commissioned them. He appeared to Thomas—a skeptical disciple—and invited him, "Put your finger here; see my hands. Reach out your hand and put it into my side. Stop doubting and believe!" Thomas' doubt sometimes shocks us. How could he, an apostle, witness to the healing of the blind, cures of lepers and raising of the dead, doubt? Yet many times we are equally guilty of asking, "Can God? Did God? Will God?" The original manuscript of the gospel of John ended at 20:30–31 which summed up the authors intent:

> Jesus did many other miraculous signs in the presence of his disciples, which are not recorded in this book. But these are written that you may believe that Jesus is the Christ, the Son of God, and that by believing you may have life in his name.

Chapter 21 is thought to be a second century addition. It records the reinstatement of Peter, and his commission to "feed my lambs," and concludes with the comment that "Jesus did many other things as well. If every one of them were written down I suppose that even the whole world would not have room for the books that would be written."

ACTS

The book of Acts is the only surviving narrative describing the beginnings of Christianity. The author was Luke, Paul's travelling companion, who also wrote the third gospel. Both books are dedicated to Theophilus, upon whose identity scholars speculate. He may have been Flavius Clemens, a cousin of Domitian executed in A.D. 96, or a wealthy and influential citizen of Antioch. The name means *lover of God*. Luke's purpose was to show that Christianity was not a subversive sect. Christ had been executed due to the hostility of the Jewish authorities, not for rebellion against Rome. The Book of Acts stresses that the Christians were not troublemakers, but loyal and hardworking citizens. The only point at which they would resist civil authority was when that authority contradicted God's explicit command or revelation. Peter, remaining submissive in attitude, refused to obey the Sanhedrin, asking them, "Whether it is right in the sight of God to listen to you rather than to God, you must judge; for we cannot but speak of what we have seen and heard," (Acts 4:19–20). Though frequently imprisoned for preaching, at no point did the apostles attempt to resist arrest or stir up rebellion. Paul boldly states, "if I have done anything wrong I do not refuse to die." The Book of Acts was written independently of the epistles with a tentative date of A.D. 85, and it is likely it was written from Rome. Acts was accepted as canonical in the later part of the second century. It provides an essential bridge between the message Jesus preached in the gospels and the account of Jesus given in the Pauline and pastoral letters. Luke may have intended to write a third book; Acts ends abruptly with Paul preaching in Rome and does not describe his mission to Spain or his and Peter's execution in A.D. 67. As in Luke's gospel the major themes are: Christianity as the new Universal religion, the power and presence of the Holy Spirit, sympathy for the poor and mild antipathy toward the rich, the role of women, and prayer and forgiveness as essential parts of the Christian life. Though Acts is filled with the persecution of the church by both the Jewish authorities and the pagans, the rapid growth of the early church is evident. In Acts 2:47 it is written of the church in Jerusalem, "the Lord added to their number daily those who were being saved." In chapter 6:7 this is redefined: "The number of disciples increased rapidly and a large number of priests became obedient to the faith." In chapter 9 we read that the church had spread throughout Judea, Galilee, and Samaria. In Antioch those dispersed by the persecution began to preach to the Greeks, and "a large number of people believed and turned to the Lord." During Paul's missionary journeys the word spread to Asia Minor (ch. 16:5), and to Europe (ch. 19:20), and eventually to Rome itself.

Acts opens with a dedication to Theophilus and moves swiftly into the description of the Ascension, with Jesus instructing his disciples, "Do not leave Jerusalem but wait for the gift my father promised." Acts 2 describes the falling of the Holy Spirit and the transformation of a bunch of frightened men into "apostles"— men who spoke with direct revelation from heaven and had the same ability as Christ to heal the lame, cure multitudes and raise the dead. Peter stepped forward as the spokesman. This unlettered fisherman was now enabled to speak with both eloquence and authority and as a result of his call to repent, 3,000 were saved that day. The power of the spirit was not limited to the miraculous speaking in tongues, nor to eloquent speech. "Everyone was filled with awe, and many wonders and miraculous signs were done by the apostles." In chapter 3, Peter's healing of the crippled beggar opened the way for him to deliver a tremendously powerful speech in Solomon's Colonnade, resulting in 5,000 being saved. This drew attention from the Sanhedrin who arrested Peter and John. Peter asserted,

> It is by the name of Jesus Christ of Nazareth, whom you crucified but whom God raised from the dead, that this man stands before you healed. He is "the stone you builders have rejected, which has become the capstone." Salvation is found in no-one else, for there is no other name under heaven given to men by which we must be saved.

The Sanhedrin conferred together, they admitted the validity of the miracle (ch. 4:6) but decided to suppress all preaching in Christ's name. They commanded Peter and John not to speak or teach in Christ's name. The apostles replied, "Judge for yourselves whether it is right in God's sight to obey you rather than God. For we cannot help speaking about what we have seen and heard." After further threats they were released. Upon their release Peter and John rejoined the others and prayed, "enable your servants to speak your word with boldness. Stretch out your hand to heal and perform miraculous signs and wonders through the name of your holy servant Jesus." After they prayed, the place where they were meeting was shaken and the Holy Spirit fell again. Chapter 5 records great crowds receiving healing. The Sadducees, filled with jealousy, arrested the apostles, but an angel released them. In the morning the apostles were standing in the temple court preaching and the guards brought them before the Sanhedrin again. The high priest reminded them that he had forbidden them to teach in Jesus' name. Peter reasserted that "we must obey God rather than men. . . . They were furious and wanted to put them to death." However, Gamiliel intervened and his wisdom prevailed: "Leave these men alone! Let them go! for if their purpose or activity is of human origin it will fail. But if it is from God, you will not be able to stop these men, you will only find yourselves fighting against God." The apostles were then flogged and released, "rejoicing because they had been counted worthy of suffering disgrace for the name." This is a New Testament theme (see Lk. 6:22 and Ja. 1:2–4), that persecution and trials are permitted to strengthen our faith, cleanse us from materialism, develop perseverance and bring us to maturity. An untested man cannot be relied upon. Chapter 6 marks a change in direction. Luke appears to be drawing from a new source which describes the growth of Hellenistic and Universal Christianity as distinct from Hebrew Christianity. As the community grew new problems arose. In this case, it was a question of administering relief. New Testament Christians took their social responsibilities seriously. As the size of the church increased and preaching and teaching duties increased the relief work was neglected. The apostles felt "it would not to be right for us to neglect the ministry of the word of God to wait on tables. Brothers choose seven men from among you who are known to be full of the spirit and wisdom. We will turn this responsibility over to them."

Stephen, a young man of great abilities, was one of the seven deacons appointed. Stephen's preaching antagonized the Hellenistic Jews who did not accept Christ. Peter and John had gotten off with a flogging, but Stephen was sentenced to be stoned to death. And though the Hebrew Christians were permitted to remain in Jerusalem, the Hellenistic believers were driven out (ch. 8:1). St. Paul—then named Saul—witnessed Stephen's death. Like Christ, Stephen prayed for his murderers (ch. 7:60). "Saul began to destroy the church, going from house to house, he

159

dragged off men and women to prison." The Christians, though fleeing for their lives, did not abandon their faith. Philip, another of the seven, led a mission in Samaria with "great signs and miracles." Peter and John were sent down to confirm the new church, but an angel sent Philip out to the desert. There he met an Ethiopian eunuch. Philip "told him the good news about Jesus," and the man joyfully accepted his savior and was baptized. Philip continued his missionary journey to Caesarea. Saul was given authority to arrest Christians and set out for Damascus when "a light from heaven flashed around him" and he heard the Lord. Saul was blinded and led into the city. In a vision the Lord spoke to a disciple named Ananias and told him to heal Saul. Ananias demurred; he knew Saul's reason for coming to Damascus! But the Lord insisted, "Go! This man is my chosen instrument to carry my name before the Gentiles and their kings!" Ananias went to Saul, healed him and baptized him. Saul spent several days being instructed then he began to preach in the synagogues that Jesus was the Son of God. As his ministry spread "the Jews conspired to kill him," but the disciples lowered him in a basket through a hole in the walls. He went to Jerusalem, but the disciples did not trust him. Barnabbas was willing to risk it! He brought Paul to the apostles. Again the Grecian Jews were most hostile to the gospel and tried to kill him. The brethren sent him back to his native Tarsus. By now the gospel had spread throughout Judea, Galilee and Samaria (ch. 9:31).

Peter was travelling and strengthening the churches. He healed a paralytic at Lydda and in Joppa raised a woman from the dead. Staying in Joppa for a few days he was to begin the first outreach to the Gentiles. Peter was praying and fell into a trance. He saw a sheet being lowered from heaven with all kinds of animals on it. The Lord told him, "Kill and eat." Peter refused. He observed the Jewish dietary laws, but the Lord told him, "Do not call anything impure that God has made clean." This happened three times. While Peter was meditating on this, messengers arrived from Cornelius. Cornelius was a centurion, who "gave generously to those in need and prayed to God regularly." An angel appeared to him and told him to send to Joppa for Simon, called Peter. The Spirit told Peter, "Do not hesitate to go with them, for I have sent them." Peter and six brothers went to Caesarea, and as Peter preached, "the Holy Spirit came on all who heard the message." Peter ordered that they be baptized and stayed with them a few days. Arriving back in Jerusalem, Peter explained what had happened and the church praised God. "So then, God has granted even the Gentiles repentance unto life." In Antioch the Hellenistic Jews began preaching to the Gentiles and the council at Jerusalem dispatched Barnabbas. Barnabbas was delighted and brought Saul from Tarsus to help him. For a year they instructed the infant church. Agabbus predicted a severe famine, so the disciples sent relief for the Judean church by Barnabbas and Paul.

Chapter 12 moves back to Jerusalem where Herod beheaded James, the brother of John, and arrested Peter. The church began to earnestly intercede for him. That night an angel appeared and freed Peter leading him outside. Herod sought him and had the unfortunate guards executed. Herod's own demise came quickly. He went to Caesarea, dressed in great pomp to address the embassies of Tyre and Sidon. When the crowd shouted, "This is the voice of a god, not a man," he accepted their homage, and was immediately struck by an angel. Josephus records that Herod had been taught to believe an owl would be the harbinger of his death. While the crowd thundered adulation he saw an owl sitting on the awning of the theater. He was seized with sudden abdominal pain and died of a loathsome disease. "But the word of God continued to increase and spread."

Barnabbas and Saul, together with Mark returned to Antioch. The spirit commanded that they be sent out. The church solemnly commissioned them and sent them out as their representatives. The remainder of the book of Acts is devoted to Paul's first three missionary journeys. Barnabbas was in charge on the first journey. Sent by the Holy Spirit they sailed to Cyprus. Travelling across Cyprus they arrived at Paphos where they encountered a sorcerer (Bar-Jesus) who opposed their preaching. Paul, filled with the spirit, inflicted physical blindness on this man who was deliberately spiritually blind. This unusual and frightening miracle, reminiscent of Peter's striking down Annanias and Saphira in chapter 5, brought about the salvation of the proconsul. Leaving Cyprus they sailed to Perga, where John Mark left them. Paul had become the acknowledged leader and spokesperson, and it was Paul who preached in the synagogue in Pisidian Antioch, warning the Jews that it is through Jesus, raised from the dead, that forgiveness of sins comes and to beware scoffing. Many of the Jews opposed Paul, who solemnly declared, "We had to speak the word of God to you first. Since you reject it and do not consider yourselves worthy of eternal life, we now turn to the Gentiles." The Gentiles were glad, "and all who were appointed for eternal life believed." Again "the Jews who refused to believe stirred up the Gentiles and poisoned their minds against the brothers." The apostles fled to Lystra. There Paul cured a lame man and the crowds began to shout, "the Gods have come down to us in human form!" and wanted to sacrifice to Paul and Barnabbas. Paul restrained them, "We too are only men, human like you. We are bringing you good news telling you to turn from these worthless things to the living God." However Jews from Antioch arrived and caused the fickle mob to stone Paul, leaving him for dead. He was not and the following day they went to Derbe where they made many disciples. "They then returned to Lystra, Iconium and Antioch, strengthening the disciples" and appointing elders. After short stops in Pisidia, Pamphylia Perga and Attalia they returned to Antioch and reported to the church.

Chapter 15 describes the council at Jerusalem in A.D. 49. With the inclusion of large numbers of non-Jewish/Gentile believers came problems. Devout Jews who stuck to the mosaic law tried to enforce circumcision on the Gentile believers. This caused sharp disputes. Paul and Barnabbas were sent to Jerusalem to get a ruling from the council. The church was in danger of splitting in two over this issue! Paul argued, "why do you try to test God by putting on the necks of the disciples a yoke that neither we nor our fathers have been able to bear? No! We believe it is through the grace of our Lord Jesus that we are saved, just as they are." The Pharisees spoke and Peter also contributed. James, as Jesus eldest surviving male relative and leader of the council, rendered the historic decision that moved Christianity into a universal faith rather than a Jewish sect:

> It is my judgement, therefore, that we should not make it difficult for the Gentiles who are turning to God. Instead we should write to them, telling them to abstain from food polluted by idols, from sexual immorality, from the meat of strangled animals and from blood.

The apostles and elders sent Judas and Silas back with Paul and Barnabbas with a letter formally enacting this decision. The letter may be read in chapter 16:23–29. After encouraging the Church at Antioch, Judas and Silas returned to Jerusalem. Paul and Barnabbas remained in Antioch preaching and teaching.

Paul decided to revisit the infant churches they has started, but he quarreled with Barnabbas, who wanted to bring John Mark with them. They parted company. Barnabbas with Mark sailed to Cyprus; Paul took Silas. Paul went north, through Syria and Cilicia and Galatia. In Lystra he was joined by Timothy. At Troas, Paul had a vision of a Macedonian man asking him to "Come over to Macedonia and help us." Luke was with Paul at this point of his journey. From Troas they sailed to Samanthrace and then to Phillipi. At Phillipi, Paul converted a woman called Lydia. She and her household were baptized and she invited the missionaries to stay at her home. Paul cast a spirit of divination out of a slave girl. Her owners were furious; this meant a great loss of income, and they had Paul and Silas arrested. After being severely flogged they were thrown into prison. About midnight Paul and Silas were praying and singing hymns. Such is the power of praise! No jail can imprison the spirit of a man whose mind is set on Christ. The earth shook and all the cell doors flew open. The jailer seeing all the doors open prepared to kill himself—he would have been executed for permitting the prisoners to escape (see chapter 12:19)—but Paul shouted, "Don't harm yourself! We are all here." The jailer was so impressed by the apostle's fearless demeanor he cried, "Sirs, what must I do to be saved." Paul summed up the gospel in a sentence, "Believe in the Lord Jesus, and you will be saved—you and your household." The jailer and his entire household accepted Christ that night. The following morning Paul and Silas were released, but asked to leave the city. They travelled to Thessalonica where Paul, again entering the synagogue, began to preach that Jesus was the Christ. The Jews formed a mob and arrested Jason (Paul's host). Jason was later released by the city officials, but the believers sent Paul and Silas off. In Berea, Paul's initial success encountered opposition when the Jews from Thessalonica arrived. Paul left for Athens, alone. There he preached at the Areopagus—the rock on which he is reputed to have stood is preserved—and preached the touching and beautiful sermon on the unknown god. Some sneered, but others believed. Paul went to Corinth where he met Priscilla and Aquilla, and there he was joined by Timothy and Silas. "Paul devoted himself exclusively to preaching, testifying to the Jews that Jesus was the Christ." When they opposed him he warned them, "Your blood will be on your own heads! I am clear of my responsibility. From now on I will go to the Gentiles." Paul stayed there a year and a half, after which the Jews arrested him and dragged him before Gallio. Gallio refused to meddle with Jewish "words and names and your own law. Settle the matter yourselves." Paul went to Ephesus where the synagogue received him favorably. From there he sailed back to Antioch. His stay at home was short. Almost immediately he set out again, travelling throughout Galatia and Phrygia strengthening the disciples. Arriving at Ephesus, he met some followers of John the Baptist and led them to salvation. Paul preached in the synagogue for three months but then rented the lecture hall of Tyrannus for two years. "All the Jews and Greeks who lived in the province of Asia heard the word of the Lord." Extraordinary miracles accompanied Paul, "even handkerchiefs and aprons that had touched him were taken to the sick, and their illnesses were cured and evil spirits left them." Many who were involved in sorcery repented and burned their scrolls publicly. "In this way the word of the Lord spread rapidly and grew in power." Demetrius, a silversmith who made shrines of Artemius, was appalled at the loss of revenue and had Paul's travelling companions Giaus and Aristarchus arrested as blasphemers. They city clerk quieted the mob. They did not want to draw attention from the Roman authorities.

Paul left for Macedonia, then travelled through Greece for three months. Arriving at Troas, Paul preached and extraordinarily long sermon in an upper room. There a young man, named Eutychus, fell asleep and fell from the third story and died. Paul raised him from the dead and continued preaching till daylight! Then he departed. At Miletus he sent for the Ephesian elders and encouraged them to "keep watch over yourselves and all the flock of which the Holy Spirit has made you overseers." He warned them that false teachers (savage wolves) would come, and to be on guard. From Miletus, Paul and his companions sailed to Tyre.

Paul was warned by prophets not to go to Jerusalem. At Caeserea also Agabbus warned him that the Jews would hand him over to the Gentiles. Paul's teaching had aroused so much hostility among the Jews that their feeling was: If Paul lived, Judaism as it had been known for centuries would die. Paul's friends warned him not to set foot in Jerusalem. But Paul had long since passed the point where his personal safety was of primary interest, and he asked, "What are you doing, weeping and breaking my heart, for I am ready not only to be imprisoned but even to die at Jerusalem for the name of the Lord Jesus." When Paul arrived at Jerusalem, James the Just—Christ's brother—welcomed him, with perhaps a little apprehension. The church at Jerusalem were respected as a Jewish sect, who other than expecting Christ to return, scrupulously followed the law. They didn't want Paul causing them problems! They asked Paul to purify himself "so everybody will know . . . you are living in obedience to the law." Paul submitted. Unfortunately, some Asian Jews seeing him incited a mob. "The whole city was aroused" and dragged Paul from the temple. The Romans prevented his death by arresting him.

Paul's attempted speech of defense in chapter 22 incited the mob yet further. They cried, "Rid the earth of him! He is not fit to live!" The following day the commander brought Paul before the Sanhedrin. There Paul cried out, "I stand on trial because of my hope in the resurrection of the dead." The Pharisees and Sadducees began to quarrel and the trial broke up. Because the Jews were determined to kill Paul, the centurion transferred Paul to Caesarea. Paul was tried before Felix, the governor. Felix postponed the trial, and Paul used the opportunity to witness to him! While not as infamous as Pilate, Felix is the unfortunate who said, "Go thy way for this time; when I have a convenient season I will call for thee." Like many who procrastinate over whether or not to grasp salvation, the convenient time never came. Two years later Felix was succeeded by Festus. When Festus asked Paul to stand trial in Jerusalem, Paul "appealed to Caesar." As a Roman citizen, Paul had the right to be tried by Caesar's representative and no other. Tired of mistrials and imprisonment, Paul demanded the case be tried before the highest authority. Festus believed in Paul's innocence. After Paul had appeared before Festus and Agrippa they both agreed, "This man is not doing anything that deserves death or imprisonment." Paul again used the trial to preach fervently. "I pray God that not only you but all who are listening to me today may become what I am except for these chains." Paul was handed over to a centurion named Julius to be brought to Rome. Shipwrecked en route on Malta, Paul healed the chief official's father. "When this happened, the rest of the sick on the island came and were cured." Eventually arriving in Rome, Paul was permitted to live in his own (rented) house under guard. Again he preached to the Jews at Rome. Some believed, but others would not. Paul warned them, "God's salvation has been sent to the Gentiles and they will listen!" For two years Paul was able, though imprisoned, to preach without hindrance. Acts ends abruptly at this point. Luke may have intended to write a third volume, or did write another book which has been lost to us. We know that Paul was released, but during the persecution of A.D. 65–67 both he and Peter were executed.

ROMANS

The book of Romans, written by the apostle Paul en route to Jerusalem, gives us the most complete picture of the gospel preached by the early church and the doctrinal beliefs it held. In jail at Phillipi, Paul had summarized the gospel: "Believe on the Lord Jesus and thou shalt be saved." In Romans, Paul shows the logical workings out of that salvation and what it entailed. A masterpiece of literature, this epistle spurred Luther to start the reformation and continues to challenge and edify the church. It deals primarily with the theme "the just shall live by faith" and compares the supremacy of faith over the law. It moves on to tell us how to fully live this new life by transforming our minds.

Paul begins his epistle stating boldly that the resurrection proved Jesus was Lord. He does not attempt to argue with the adoptonist views of current Rome (that Christ was adopted as God's son on the cross). He merely states, "Through the spirit of holiness he was declared with power to be the Son of God by his resurrection from the dead, Jesus Christ our Lord." Paul states that the gospel is dynamos; it is power! Power to save us fully, power to make us righteous, power to transform us into "living sacrifices." God does not grade on the curve; we are either 100% righteous or we not righteous at all. This righteousness is imputed to us through faith in Christ Jesus (ch. 5:19). It is a righteousness apart from the law; it supercedes the law! By the law no man can become righteous. "It is not those who hear the law who are righteous in God's sight, but it is those who obey the law," and no man has fully kept the law. The whole thrust of chapter 2 is to shock the "righteous" out of their complacency. Jews, having the law and failing to keep it, will be judged by the Gentiles, who not having the law but following their conscience keep the law.

Gentiles, though not having the law, do not escape judgement. They will not be judged by the law but by their reason and conscience. In chapter 1:19–20, Paul states that creation itself testifies to the fact that there *is* a creator. "Since the creation of the world, God's invisible qualities—his eternal power and divine nature have been carefully seen." The only way men can fail to see this is by deliberately repressing this knowledge. The Greek terms Paul uses imply deliberately killing this living knowledge. When men refuse to accept this instinctive knowledge, their minds and hearts become darkened. This leads to a woeful state. Unfortunately Romans 1:26–32 can be seen fulfilled in our daily newspaper. When men abandon God they eventually abandon all moral precepts. Paul springs a trap on the unwary reader. As we condemn the foolish Gentile heathen, Paul cries, "You, therefore, have no excuse—at whatever point you judge the other you are condemning yourself, because you who pass judgement do the same things." Our hearts' hardness is dealt with in chapters 2–4, Paul proving conclusively that by ourselves we cannot fully keep the law; it is only through faith, God's grace, that we are saved. "Therefore, since we have been justified through faith we have peace with God through Jesus." Paul goes on to argue that just as through Adam's sin death entered the world, through Christ's resurrection we "receive God's abundant provision of grace . . . righteousness . . ." and "justification." We are given spiritual life, a new life. Through baptism we are symbolically and spiritually crucified with Christ; our old man is put to death and through the holy spirit we are given the ability to live without sin. Though we still struggle daily with sin, our struggle is no longer a hopeless one. We have the power of God working within us to be "set free from sin and become slaves to God." Chapter 7 is devoted to our struggle with sin. In our mind we long to obey God's law, but we sin. Chapters 8 and 12 tell us how to overcome sin. Like most spiritual battles it begins in the mind. "The mind of the sinful man is death, but the mind controlled by the spirit is life and peace; the sinful mind is hostile to God. It does not submit to God's law nor can it do so," (ch. 8:6). Paul continues this theme in Chapter 12:2. "Do not conform any longer to the pattern of this world, but be transformed by the renewing of your mind. Then you will be able to test and approve what God's will is, his good, pleasing and perfect will." In chapter 13 he urges, "Do not think about how to gratify the desires of the sinful nature." If we set our minds on God, we will be more than conquerors.

Chapters 9–11 involve an argument about predestination and God's sovereign choice. Jewish theologians did not have the trouble with the concept that we do. God has freedom of choice! We are so concerned about our rights, we often forget God's. He lives, he makes choices. We feel that if a man is predestined for salvation or damnation his actions have no bearing on the matter. But the Jews accepted both God's sovereign choice and man's moral responsibility. Because you are the elect you must live worthily of that calling, election is a responsibility, not a show of favoritism. Paul reminds us abruptly that we are the creature—God the creator! "Who are you, O man, to talk back to God? Shall what is formed say to him who formed it 'why did you make me like this.' "

The thrust of Chapters 9–11 is also a grave warning: Our election can be forfeited by negligence, as was Israel's! Chapters 9:30 through 10:21 show that though God is sovereign and has all rights over us, his creation, he does not make a one time final arbitrary decision. We are free agents and our actions towards him may move him to mercy, or we can voluntarily reject his favor!

We must not take divine blessing for granted. In chapter 12 Paul moves on to tell the elect how to live, as living sacrifices, given over daily to the will of God. Exercise your spiritual gifts. Love and honor each other, "as far as it depends on you live at peace with everyone." Chapter 13 causes many men to choke! Paul was writing during the reign of Nero, a bloodthirsty madman, yet he commanded, "Everyone must submit himself to the governing authorities for their is no authority except that which God has established. The authorities that exist have been established by God." A similar note is heard in I Peter 2:13. We are to submit, even to tyrants. Normally rulers punish evil men, not good men. However, even if we suffer unjustly we must submit. God will eventually deal with the oppressor. Satan's chief sin is argued about: pride? or rebellion? or pride leading to rebellion? All attempts to usurp authority come from Satan. God will exalt the righteous (if they submit and wait patiently); he will humble the proud. The only point at which we may disobey lawful authority is when it conflicts with God's commands. Chapter 14 is a reiteration of the great truth revealed to Peter in Acts 10: nothing is of itself unclean. The dietary and social laws are now superseded as "the kingdom of God is not a matter of eating and drinking but of righteousness, peace and joy in the Holy Spirit." Do not argue about the minutiae of Law observance. "We who are strong ought to bear with the failings of the weak." We are urged to put unity as a priority. Paul closes the epistle saying he plans a mission to Spain, which is not documented in the New Testament. On this journey he hoped to visit Rome. The book ends with several personal greetings and a brief prayer glorifying God.

I CORINTHIANS

I Corinthians was written from Ephesus, by the apostle Paul to the church at Corinth in A.D. 54 or 55. The Corinthian church had been established by Paul and Silvanus in A.D. 50–51. Although it was a strong church numerically and the wealthiest and most influential of the Greek churches, it was a church riddled with division and strife. It was a church in which licentious was common, a church where drunkenness and greed were manifest at the Lord's Supper. Paul's letter is disciplinarian rather than doctrinal.

Paul tackled the party divisions first, demanding, "Is Christ divided? Was Paul crucified for you?" Paul, Cephas (Peter) and Apollos are "only servants, through whom you came to believe." Paul laid the foundation of the church; Apollo built upon it; but it is the spirit that brings men to salvation. "My message and my preaching were not with wise and persuasive words but with a demonstration of the spirit's power, so that your faith might not rest on man's wisdom but on God's power." In fact, the wisdom of the world is incompatible with the revelation of the spirit. Paul was preparing to send Timothy to the Corinthians to remind them of the basis of their salvation. He then dealt with a specific problem which had arisen in the church: incest. Corinth was devoted to the worship of Aphrodite, the goddess of sex. Some of this thinking had crept into the church (chapter 6:12–20 deals very strongly with those who see sex as an act as amoral as eating).

Chapter 5 deals with a specific case of incest. Paul demands the expulsion of the guilty party, possibly to shock him into repentance. Paul's tirade against sexual immorality in chapter 6 moves into a discussion about marriage and divorce in chapter 7. Paul considered the single state preferable. A single person can devote all their energy to the Lord's service, while a married man or woman must always consider their partner, even if their partner is not a believer. A believer may only separate from the unbeliever if the unbeliever leaves them. Paul's strong emphasis on the desirability of the single state was partly due to his conviction that the Second Coming was imminent. He was not however an aesthetic; he did not attempt to say that marriage was sin. In fact he said married couples were not to deprive each other of their conjugal rights.

Paul's next concern was food sacrificed to idols. The letter from the council at Jerusalem (Acts 15:19f) told believing Gentiles to abstain from food polluted by idols. The Corinthian church was being divided over this issue. Some Christians demanded their rights to eat as they saw fit, but others were "still so accustomed to idols that when they eat such food they think of it as having been sacrificed to an idol, and since their conscience is weak it is defiled." Paul urges the stronger Christians to forgo their liberty lest it causes the weaker believers to fall. "If what I eat causes my brother to fall into sin, I will never eat meat again, so that I will not cause him to fall." Paul urges the church to seek to build each other up (ch. 10:24), warns against any compromise with idolatry (verses 14–22), and admonishes that we must be vigilant lest we lapse into sin (verses 11–12).

The incidents of greed and drunkenness at the Lord's Supper are firmly dealt with in chapter 11, together with a strong warning that we must be morally prepared when we come to the Lord's Table. Otherwise sickness and death will follow. Chapter 12 lists all the spiritual gifts available to the church. These gifts are for the edification of the body. We, as individuals are a part of the body. Paul uses the parable of the body to illustrate our interdependence on each other and to urge unity. Paul urges believers to seek the greatest spiritual gifts but warned that without love all these gifts mean nothing. Love is not an emotion; it is a mental attitude, a decision of the will to seek the well being of others. Chapter 13 describes God's self sacrificing love. This is the kind of love we are to show to each other.

> Love is patient, love is kind. It does not envy, it does not boast, it is not proud. It is not rude, it is not self-seeking, it is not easily angered, it keeps no record of wrongs. Love does not delight in evil but rejoices with the truth. It always protects, always trusts, always hopes, always perseveres. Love never fails.

In chapter 14 Paul addresses excesses in worship. The acid test for what is appropriate in public worship is given in verses 12 and 26: Does it build up the body? Believers are urged to give place to each other that all may participate and all be built up. Chapter 11 verses 2–16 and chapter 14:34–35 offend many ladies. In chapter 14 the apostle commands women to keep quiet in church. Some theologians believe these verses to be an editorial gloss. They do not seem to fit in with Paul's devotion and gratitude (and indebtedness) to Lydia and Priscilla, and contradict his injunction in chapter 11 that women are allowed to pray and prophesy with the stipulation that their hair is covered. Others explain this passage thus: Men and women were segregated; the women sat at the back. Unable to hear clearly, they would call out to their husbands, and this shouting back and forth was both disruptive and unseemly. In chapter 11 women are plainly told they are subordinate to men, woman was created for man, not man for woman.

Women are told to cover their head while praying or prophesying. At the time this epistle was written only courtesans went unveiled in public, so Paul was adhering to the social traditions of the day. Verse 10 causes controversy. Women are told to cover their heads lest they tempt the angels. One possible interpretation is that angels uphold God's authority and his chain of command is:

GOD
CHRIST
MAN
WOMAN

A woman covering her head shows her voluntary submission to God's order and so will not incur the angels wrath. Others have suggested these are fallen angels and women must beware of arousing their lust! Few modern churches still maintain this custom.

Chapter 15 reproclaims the resurrection. The resurrection is the heart of the Christian gospel. If the resurrection did not occur the apostles are liars and the believer's faith is vain. "If Christ has not been raised, your faith is futile; you are still in your sins." Paul has no room for a gospel that tries to ignore eternity. Christ lives, through him we shall rise (ch. 15:23) with a heavenly body (verse 51); we shall rule with him! Paul glowingly describes the rapture: The dead shall rise, we shall be transformed and have a heavenly/spiritual body. Because we have this hope we can stand firm.

Chapter 16 closes with personal greetings. Verse 13 sums up the epistle: "Be on your guard; stand firm in the faith; be men of courage; be strong. Do everything in love."

II CORINTHIANS

II Corinthians was the fourth letter written by the apostle Paul to the Corinthian church. A lost letter was written urging them to refrain from sexual immorality (this letter is referred to in I Corinthians 5:19). I Corinthians dealt with the party spirit and specific discipline problems in the church. Paul then sent Timothy to Corinth, but his visit was unsuccessful in restoring discipline. Jewish Christians arriving with letters of commendation (II Cor. 3:1) demanded positions of leadership and turned the church against Paul. Paul revisited Corinth to try to restore order and was not very successful. He wrote a third stern letter from Ephesus. Titus appears to have delivered this letter. Using it—together with Paul's loyal supporters—he restored order and the church repented (II Cor. 3:1). The rebellious leader was forced to leave the church. Once Paul was assured that true repentance had occurred he urged the Corinthians to forgive the offenders. II Corinthians is a letter of restoration, Paul thanking God and delighting in the restoration of proper relationships between himself and this church. A probable date for this letter is A.D. 55–57.

Paul began the letter asserting his own authority and calling of God: "Paul an apostle of Christ Jesus by the will of God . . ." The church itself is his letter of recommendation (ch. 3:3). In chapters 10–12 he gives his spiritual qualifications and warns the Corinthians against "super apostles" who elevate their own learning boastfully and end up enslaving and exploiting the church (11v20). Ironically Paul uses suffering as a measure of true Christianity rather than eloquence of preaching. Suffering causes us to trust more and more in God, "that we might rely not on our own selves but on God who raises the dead." Our troubles and trials have the primary purpose of causing us to fix our eyes on God (ch. 3:17–18).

Chapters 8 and 9 refer to the collection for relief of the saints in Judea. Paul is scrupulous to show that this collection is not for his benefit. In fact he has taken no wages from the Corinthian Church. It is intended to help edify the church. The Gentiles are to give not only out of compassion but out of a sense of spiritual debt to the Judean church. The Judean church will in turn see the love and Christ-like spirit of the Gentiles through this generosity. Paul knew it would be at risk of his own life that he brought this gift to Judea, but church unity was a great priority to him. Paul shows the superiority of the new covenant over that of Sinai (ch. 2:7–9). The reconciliation brought about by God through Christ makes us new creatures. "If anyone is in Christ, he is a new creation; the old has gone, the new has come," (II Cor. 5:20). Because we are made righteous by faith, we are urged to "purify ourselves from everything that contaminates body and spirit, perfecting holiness out of reverence for God," (ch. 7:1). Paul urges the Corinthians to avoid the immorality prevalent in that cosmopolitan city. "Do not be yoked together with unbelievers. . . . What does a believer have in common with an unbeliever? What agreement is there between the temple of God and idols." In chapter 10 he goes further; we are not only to avoid sin, we are to "demolish arguments and everything that sets itself up against the knowledge of God, and we take captive every thought to make it obedient to Christ." We are to manifest outwardly that spiritual life which was given to us as a gift from God. The way to do this, to live victoriously, is by setting it in our will, giving no place to any thought or opinion that is not in harmony with the gospel, "taking captive every thought" and "aiming for perfection," (ch. 13:11).

GALATIANS

Galatians has been compared to a religious Magna Carta. It was written from Ephesus to Galatia during Paul's third missionary journey in A.D. 52–53. It proclaims our freedom from the law and total dependence on Christ. Paul shows that man cannot win God's favor by works. Obedience to the law will not bring salvation; only faith in Christ brings salvation. Paul argues that grace was always God's plan—the promise to Abraham was given 430 years before Moses received the law. The law was given to convince men that they cannot save themselves and to point them to Christ (ch. 3:1–22). If salvation were possible through the law Christ died for nothing (ch. 2:21). This freedom from the law is not license to sin. Through Christ you are charged to "live by the spirit and you will not gratify the desires of the sinful nature." Chapter 5:22 lists the fruit of a life led by the Holy Spirit:

> The fruit of the spirit is love, joy, peace, patience, kindness, faithfulness, gentleness and self-control. Against such things there is no law. Those who belong to Christ have crucified the sinful nature and its passions and desires.

Paul urges the Galatians to "sow to please the spirit." This is done by doing good to all (ch. 6:10) and by loving our neighbors (ch. 5:14), carrying each others burdens (ch. 6:2). Paul claims that those who accept Christ and live in the spirit, like Isaac, are children of the promise and the true Israel. Anyone who tries to preach otherwise is perverting the gospel. Paul is amazed that the Galatians who embraced the faith so eagerly are so easily swayed to a doctrine of legalism. Paul closes, "Neither circumcision nor uncircumcision means anything, what counts is a new creation. Peace and mercy to all who follow this rule, even to the Israel of God."

EPHESIANS

Some theologians question Paul's authorship of Ephesians, others accept Paul's authorship but believe the epistle was written to the church at Ladocia. The early church accepted Paul's authorship and used this epistle on a regular basis. It is a prison epistle probably written at the same time as Colossians and Philemon, during Paul's final imprisonment in Rome. The central theme is unity. God designed man to be united under Christ, "to bring all things in heaven and on earth together under one head," (ch. 1:10). Already Christ has abolished the enmity between Jew and Gentile making them one. "The Gentiles are heirs together with Israel, members together of one body, and sharers together in the promise of Christ Jesus." Through him we have access to God, we the church "are being built together to become a dwelling in which God lives by his spirit." Through this establishment of God's kingdom on earth in the church, it is God's intention to bring all men to salvation. Chapters 1–3 develop this theme. Chapters 4-6 explain the practical implications for us as individuals in the church, in society, in the family and in our struggle against "spiritual forces of evil." In the church, God has given apostles, prophets, evangelists, pastors, and teachers "to prepare God's people for works of service," that we may become mature, filled with the fullness of Christ. We are to be gentle, patient, and humble, filled with love. We are to be one in Christ, moving and living as he directs and guides. In society we are to "put off" our sinful desires. We are to be truthful, forgiving, guarding our speech. "Get rid of all bitterness, rage and anger, brawling and slander, along with every form of malice. Be kind and compassionate." We must above all be thankful to God. In the family wives are told to submit to their husbands as the church submits to Christ. Husbands are to love their wives as Christ loved the church. Children must be obedient. Fathers must not exasperate their children but bring them up in the training and instruction of the Lord. Slaves must similarly obey their masters, as though service rendered to the master was being rendered to Christ. Masters are to remember their heavenly master and act appropriately.

Chapter 6:10–20 describe the armor of God. Our struggle is not against flesh and blood but against "the powers of this dark world and against the spiritual forces of evil in the heavenly realms." (It is vital to remember this when dealing with "wicked" men.) We are to put on the armor of God that we may be able to stand firm. We are to put on truth, righteousness, the gospel of peace, the shield of faith, the helmet of salvation and wield the sword of the spirit. And we must pray continually. Prayer is our lifeline and we must defend it. Being armored and alert is essential to victory in the Christian walk. Truth—reality as God sees it—will keep us from sin. The righteousness of Christ will protect us from the enemies accusations. Concerning the gospel of peace: men long for peace, but only in Christ can true peace be found. This peace must destroy all false peace and halfway houses at which men seek comfort. Faith will enable us to withstand temptation; as Christ is all sufficient, nothing this world has to offer will draw us from him. The helmet of salvation symbolizes divine protection. The sword of the spirit, the word of God is our only offensive weapon. With the word of God we evangelize, and "fearlessly make known the mystery of the gospel." We renew our minds and build up our churches.

Paul closes with a benediction to the brethren, wishing them peace, love faith and grace.

PHILIPPIANS

Philippians is one of the seven prison epistles written by Paul from Rome, possibly dated A.D. 64, shortly before his martyrdom. It was carried by Epaphroditus back to his native Phillipi. This is one of the most intimate epistles written by Paul. Here we find no swelling theological arguments. It is pervaded with joy. Paul is looking beyond this life and into heaven. The Philippian church had remained loyal to Paul throughout the years when the other churches—influenced by Jewish Christians—had turned their backs on him. Paul remembered this loyalty with thankfulness. Paul did not accept wages from any church, but he joyfully accepted the Philippians love-gifts during his imprisonment and earlier. They were the first church established in Europe and the most loyal. They too had personality conflicts, but it is with the utmost gentleness that Paul pleads with Euodia and Syntyche to be reconciled.

Though Paul does not give reasoned arguments, his theology is stated more clearly in Philippians than in many longer letters. The whole argument of faith versus works, labored over in Romans, is summed up in a single verse, chapter 3:9. Paul has learned true contentment and endeavors to share this secret with his friends. No psychological or theological textbook can give sounder advice than is found in Philippians chapter 4:6–8:

Do not be anxious about anything, but in everything, by prayer and petition, with thanksgiving, present your requests to God. And the peace of God, which transcends all understanding, will guard your hearts and your minds in Christ Jesus. Finally brothers, whatever is true, whatever is noble, whatever is right, whatever is pure, whatever is lovely, whatever is admirable—if anything is excellent or praiseworthy—think about such things.

If we can set our minds like Paul, we will be able to look beyond our circumstances however dire. We will know Christ is sufficient (ch. 4:19). Imprisoned, knowing some of his detractors are enjoying shredding his reputation (ch. 1:15), Paul can ask, "What does it matter? The important thing is that in every way, whether from false motives or true, Christ is preached." Even death holds no terrors for "to live is Christ, to die is gain."

COLOSSIANS

Written from Rome during Paul's final imprisonment, this epistle is closely related to both Philemon and Ephesians. All three were to be delivered by Tychius who was accompanied by the former runaway slave Onesimus. Colossians was written to halt the spread of a "mystery cult" growing up in the church. Epaphras had preached the gospel of Christ's sufficiency and had Paul's full support (ch. 1:7), but this simple gospel was being challenged by "hollow and deceptive philosophy," (ch. 2:5). This philosophy included worship of angels and cultic regulations possibly related to Judaism. Paul warns that "such regulations have indeed an appearance of wisdom, with their self-imposed worship, their false humility and their harsh treatment of the body, but they lack any real value in restraining sensual indulgence." Rather than submitting to complicated rules and regulations, we are to "set (our) hearts on things above." We are to put to death our sin nature, ridding ourselves of anger, malice, slander, filthy language and lies, and we must love each other. From this general guidance Paul moves to specifics. Wives are to submit to their husbands; children submit to parents; husbands are to love their wives; fathers are to handle their children with wisdom. Slaves are to serve their masters wholeheartedly, and their masters are to be fair remembering their master! Paul urges faithfulness and vigilance in prayer.

The epistle closes recommending Tychius and Onesimus, and with personal greetings. Paul urges the Colossians to read the now lost Laodicean epistle (some scholars hold that this is our Ephesian epistle), and the Laodiceans are to read the Colossian epistle.

Archippus is encouraged to complete his work. Paul signed the epistle both to authenticate it and convey his personal regards. The sad phrase "remember my chains' appeals for prayer and urges obedience. See how much the faith has cost me! Be faithful!

I THESSALONIANS

Paul, Silvanus, and Timothy, arriving at Thessalonica after their imprisonment in Phillipi, immediately began to preach the word. Some Jews and a large number of Greeks accepted Christ, but the Jews formed a mob and dragged Paul's host, Jason, before the city officials. The disciples prevented Paul from intervening. Jason was released and Paul and Silas departed quietly in the night. Paul's departure did not end the persecution for the Christians at Thessalonica. Despite this the Thessalonian believers stood firm, "you became a model to all the believers in Macedonia and Achaia." Paul writing from Corinth in A.D. 50–51 is encouraging the infant church and rejoicing in the good report brought back by his messenger Timothy.

The Jews have no doubt slandered Paul, as a defensive note can be seen in chapter 2, where he reminds the Thessalonians of "how holy, righteous and blameless we were." In chapter 4, Paul turns to ethical demands. The Thessalonians lived in a region devoted to fertility cults. Paul reminds them, "it is God's will that you should be sanctified: that you should avoid sexual immorality. . . . God did not call us to be impure, but to live a holy life." He urges brotherly love and hard work. Since Paul's departure, some brethren had died and the church was anxious lest the dead lose their place in the kingdom. Paul comforts them. When the Lord returns the dead shall rise and "we will be caught up together with them in the clouds to meet the Lord in the air."

He urges them not to worry about the exact day of the Lord's return but to be alert and self-controlled, to live for Christ. Paul orders the idle to work and exhorts forgiveness and mutual edification. After praying that God will sanctify them—body, soul, and spirit—he reminds them, "The one who calls you is faithful and he will do it." He closes, wishing the grace of Christ upon them.

II THESSALONIANS

There had arisen the rumor or teaching that the Day of the Lord had arrived. The Thessalonian Christians were anxious, and this second letter was written to settle this matter. Paul reminded the Thessalonians that before the Second Coming the man of lawlessness (the antichrist) will arise. He will possess great power and set himself up to be worshiped. His counterfeit miracles, signs and wonders will cause many to be lead astray. Those who have not believed the truth will be enslaved. Paul has already taught the Thessalonians about this, so he moves along rapidly, thanking God that despite their persecutions the Thessalonians are standing firm. He requests prayer for protection, and that "the message of the Lord may spread rapidly and be honored." Once again he commands the idlers and busybodies to "settle down and earn the bread they eat." After praying for peace for the church, Paul signs the letter, perhaps to authenticate it, so they will know this letter—unlike the forgery mentioned in chapter 2:2—is genuine.

I TIMOTHY

Some theologians doubt the authenticity of the pastoral epistles. As evidence they cite difference of tone and word usage, and claim the epistles are of second century origin. It is hard to date this epistle; A.D. 61 has been suggested. Paul is writing to encourage Timothy, who has been his disciple and able co-worker since their meeting in Derbe and Lystra during Paul's second missionary journey.

Paul is concerned with establishing church orthodoxy. His main purpose is to encourage Timothy and to urge him to rid the church of unchristian beliefs and practices. Timothy is warned not to entertain false teachers but to hold firmly to the gospel entrusted to him. Paul gives the beginning of a liturgy: pray for those in authority (ch. 2:1–2), read scripture aloud (ch. 4:13), preach, teach, and allow the operation of the spirit.

Paul lays down the qualifications required of those seeking position in the church. Overseers/bishops must be:

> above reproach, the husband of but one wife, temperate, self-controlled, respectable, hospitable, able to teach, not given to drunkenness, not violent but gentle, not quarrelsome, not a lover of money. He must manage his own household well.

The qualifications for deacons are still strict but not quite as demanding. The wives of those in authority must also be self-controlled, trustworthy and not gossips! Paul warns Timothy, as he warned the Thessalonians, that in the last days a spirit of lawlessness and false religion will be found. Timothy is to be careful. "Watch your life and doctrine closely."

Chapter 5 gives advice on helping those who really are in need. Christians must accept responsibility for family members. "If anyone does not provide for his own, and especially for his immediate family, he has denied the faith and is worse than an unbeliever." While warning about the dangers of the love of money, Paul does not insist that Christianity is a religion for the poor only, rather that we are God's stewards and must use money rightly.

> Command those who are rich in this present world
> not to be arrogant, not to put their hope in wealth,
> which is so uncertain, but to put their hope in God
> who richly provides us with everything for our
> enjoyment. Command them to do good, to be rich
> in good deeds, to be generous and willing to share.
>
> I Timothy 6:17

In closing Paul again admonishes Timothy to guard the gospel and avoid both gnosticism (a heresy of "hidden knowledge" popular in the early church) and godless chatter.

II TIMOTHY

This epistle was written during Paul's final imprisonment. Paul had been condemned by Nero, but rejoiced that he had "finished the race. I have kept the faith. . . . Now there is in store for me the crown of righteousness which the Lord, the righteous judge will award to me." Paul has been deserted by all but Luke and longs to see his friend again, not just for his own sake but that he may encourage Timothy. The epistle is full of exhortation to the young man to stand firm. He is to testify boldly (ch. 1:8), guard the gospel entrusted to him (verse 14), be strong (ch. 2:1), appoint reliable teachers (verse 2), and endure hardship(verse 3). Further, he is to keep reminding others of their calling (2:14), study the word diligently (verse 15), continue in the tradition he has learned (ch. 3:14), and preach the word (ch. 4:2). He is also given practical warning and advice: avoid godless chatter (2:16), flee the evil desires of youth (ch. 3:1). Timothy must beware of Alexander the metalworker (ch. 4:14). He is not to be dismayed by Paul's suffering; everyone who follows Christ will be persecuted (ch. 3:12).

Though largely concerned with strengthening Timothy, Paul dwells on the last days. "There will be terrible times in the last days. People will be lovers of themselves, lovers of money, boastful, proud, abusive, disobedient to their parents, ungrateful, unholy, unforgiving . . . lovers of pleasure rather than lovers of

God—having a form of Godliness, but denying its power." When the churches—fearing the loss of members—condone lifestyles clearly denounced in the bible, and when we see "evil men and impostors go from bad to worse, deceiving and being deceived" (ch. 3:13), we cannot doubt these days have arrived.

Paul's word to us is, as it was to Timothy, "Do not be ashamed to testify about Our Lord, join with me in suffering for the gospel by the power of God who has saved us and called us to a holy life," (ch. 1:8–9). "Guard the good deposit that was entrusted to you—guard it with the help of the Holy Spirit," (ch. 1:14).

TITUS

Titus, a Gentile, accompanied Paul to Jerusalem. He was used as an illustration of the spirit's manifestation among the Gentiles (Gal. 2:1–3). He was the messenger sent by Paul to Corinth, who bearing Paul's "severe letter" won that church back to Paul. He also collected the offering at Corinth that Paul was to bring to Jerusalem. Traditionally he was the first bishop of Crete. Paul calls him "my true child in a common faith." Titus was completely loyal to Paul, proving to be a great comfort to the apostle (II Cor. 7:5–6).

Those who claim that the pastoral epistles are of second century origin believe that the epistles to Timothy reflect the character needed in a bishop in an organized community, while Titus is the supreme example of a bishop in a largely unevangelized area.

Paul had visited Crete during his first missionary journey and established churches. These churches were full of "many rebellious people, mere talkers and deceivers." Titus must silence them; he must rebuke them sharply, giving no place to myths or legalism. Titus is to warn a divisive person twice, after that "have nothing to do with him." Paul repeats a lot of the injunctions given to Timothy regarding the character traits believers must display: self-control, humility, purity of lifestyle and speech. Chapter 3:14 sums up our responsibilities in this world. "Our people must learn to devote themselves to doing what is good, in order that they may provide for daily necessities and not live unproductive lives."

PHILEMON

The letter to Philemon, covering barely a page, is one of the seven Pauline letters whose authenticity is unquestionable. On the surface it is simple: Paul met and converted Onesimus, a runaway slave. As Onesimus was under a moral obligation to return to his master, Paul sent Onesimus, accompanied by Tychius back to Collosea. This letter is Paul's personal plea to Philemon, his master, to forgive him. It is a prison epistle, either from his imprisonment in Ephesus or his final imprisonment in Rome.

Paul asks Philemon to do more than forgive Onesimus; Paul asks that the slave may be returned to Paul to help him in his ministry (verse 13). He is described as "a dear brother . . . he has become useful both to you and to me." Paul calls him "my very heart." Paul undertakes to pay Philemon for whatever wrongs the slave had previously done (verse 19). That Paul's plea was successful we know from a letter of Ignatius in A.D. 110. Onesimus, Paul's able deacon, was the Ephesian bishop who visited Ignatius on his way to trial and martyrdom in Rome! Ironically Ignatius, like Paul, was to request that an able slave, Barhus, be given to him. The letter he wrote to Onesimus closely parallels that written by Paul on Onesimus behalf! Philemon, the master, was later to publish a collection of the apostle's letters in Ephesus and this explains both the inclusion of this personal note and its historic importance.

HEBREWS

The authorship of Hebrews is unknown. Some attribute it to St. Paul, others to Barnabbus or Philo of Alexandria. Nevertheless, this book was accepted as canonical by the early church and quoted from in I Clement (A.D. 96c). The dating of the epistle is also questionable; as no mention of the fall of Jerusalem is made it was probably before A.D. 70.

Two main theories have been put forward to explain the writing of Hebrews. Either the author was combating a gnostic heresy based on Jewish tradition, or it was to prevent Jewish Christians from falling back into Judaism. The main theme of Hebrews is that Jesus is the final and perfect revelation of God; all prior revelation is superseded. "The son is the radiance of God's glory, and the exact representation of his being," (ch. 1:3). Christ is superior to the angels (ch.1:2b) and to Moses (ch. 3:1–6a). He is a priest forever (ch. 5:6); his priesthood is superior to the Levitical (ch. 7:1–28); through his sacrifice we have been forgiven (ch. 10:18) and made holy (verse 10). Though he is the perfect son of God, he became man and identified with us in our struggles. "He was in all points tempted like as we are, yet without sin . . . he himself has suffered, being tempted he is able to help them that are tempted." Christ was made perfect through suffering (ch. 2:10) and is able to bring us to perfection (ch. 7:25). We must not be afraid of suffering and must be ready to resist sin, even if it means our death (chs. 10:36–37 and 11:4). Suffering will bring us to maturity and into closer fellowship with Christ. In chapter 11, the great chapter on faith, many heroes of faith are named. We are exhorted to strive like them. "Let us lay aside every weight that doth so easily beset us and let us run with patience the race that is set before us—looking unto Jesus the author and finisher of our faith; who for the joy that was set before him endured the cross."

The superiority of the new covenant over the old is stressed. Many Israelites died in the desert due to sin (ch. 4:17–19), but Christ can "save us to the uttermost." And through the new covenant "I will put my laws into their mind and write them in their hearts, and I will be to them a God and they shall be my people." Christ purges us from dead works to serve the living God. Through him we are sanctified (ch. 10:10) and enter a new and living way (verse 20). The author warns of the gravity of neglecting or falling away from this salvation (chs. 2:3 and 10:29), and urges his readers to remember that the just shall live by faith (ch. 10:38).

Practical advice is also given. We are to stay in fellowship (ch. 10:25) and to pursue peace and holiness (ch. 12:14). We are to do good and share (ch. 3:16) and be submissive to authority (ch. 13:17). The epistle closes with a benediction:

> May the God of peace, who through the blood of the eternal covenant brought back from the dead our Lord Jesus, that great shepherd of the sheep, equip you with everything good for doing his will, and may he work in us what is pleasing to him through Jesus Christ, to whom be glory forever and ever amen.

JAMES

Traditionally attributed to James the Just, the brother of Jesus and leader of the council in Jerusalem, this epistle is one of practical advice rather than theological arguments. James does not deride faith, but explains that inward faith must express itself in outward deeds, otherwise it is questionable if faith exists. Even the demons believe there is but one God. If you see a brother or sister in need, meet them at the point of their need. Abraham (the great hero of faith) is used as an example. "His faith and his actions were working together and his faith was made complete by what he did."

James, later condemned by the Sanhedrin to be stoned (A.D. 60–62?), wrote to Jewish Christians under pressure to return to orthodox Judaism. James wrote,

> Consider it pure joy whenever you face trials of many kinds, because you know that the testing of your faith develops perseverance. Perseverance must finish its work so that you may be mature and complete not lacking anything.

It is God's will that perseverance through trials purifies us and strengthens us so that we will "receive the crown of life." However, if we yield to our evil desires/sin nature we will sin and sin brings death. We are urged to resist the devil and he will flee from us. There is a reason many of our prayers go unanswered: "You ask with wrong motives, that you spend what you get on your pleasures."

Favoritism is forbidden as is boasting and trusting in this world's goods. James urges us to "keep a tight reign on our tongue." It is "untamable—a restless evil, full of deadly poison." It is not fitting that we both praise God and curse men. "Out of the same mouth come praise and cursing this should not be." We are to seek God's wisdom, not the wisdom of this world. James shows clearly the difference between the two. Envy and selfish ambition, disorder and evil deeds are devil inspired, "but the wisdom that comes from heaven is first of all pure, then peace-loving, considerate, submissive, full of mercy and good fruit, impartial and sincere."

I PETER

I Peter, like Mark was written to a church facing martyrdom. It is filled with courage and hope based on the living God who raised Jesus from the dead. Peter's teaching is unquestioned. The polished Greek belongs to Silvanus/Silas who is acting as his scribe. The epistle was probably written from Rome CA.D. 62 before the first major persecution. Peter deals with the question of unjust suffering. We are exhorted to live godly lives so that we will not suffer as criminals. If we are persecuted for being a Christian, then "those who suffer according to God's will should commit themselves to their faithful creator and continue to do good." Peter goes further and says we were called to suffer (ch. 2:21). We are called to break the cycle of evil. "Do not repay evil with evil or insult with insult but with blessing because to this you were called," (ch. 3:9). Returning good for evil on a consistent basis will halt Satan's schemes and prevent him having any toehold in our lives. Patience, endurance, and steadfast pursuit of godliness will win the pagan (ch. 3:12) and silence their accusations (ch. 3:16). We are to be holy (ch. 1:13), ridding ourselves "of all malice and deceit, hypocrisy, envy, slander of every kind." The moral teaching of I Peter is summed up in chapter 2:17: "Live as servants of God show proper respect to everyone: Love the brotherhood of believers, fear God, honor the king."

Peter urges us to be alert and vigilant as our enemy, the devil, is continually seeking to destroy us. If we stand firm, God will strengthen us and restore us. "Cast all your anxiety on him for he cares for you." We are urged to respect those placed in authority over us, both in the world and in the church. The theological message is summed up in chapter 1:9: The goal of our faith is the salvation of our souls. Keeping this in view, the trials we face cannot harm, but will strengthen our faith. We are to aim to arm ourselves with the same attitude of Christ that we may live, not for human desires but for the will of God. If we set apart Christ as Lord we will be freed from the fear of man.

II PETER

The authenticity of II Peter has been questioned because of stylistic differences with I Peter. Some scholars feel that Peter's name was used to lend authority to the epistle, as Peter signified original authoritative Christianity. The author knew and accepted Paul's letters. He borrowed extensively from Jude and was familiar with the synoptic gospel accounts and John 21. He appears to condemn Marcion (CA.D. 144). It is believed this epistle was written from Rome in the middle of the second century. It was written "to stimulate you to wholesome thinking." Peter asks, "what kind of people ought you to be?" and answers, "You ought to live holy and godly lives. . . . make every effort to be found spotless, blameless and at peace." The divine assurance Peter has is that through the knowledge of God and Christ we have grace, peace, and everything we need for life and godliness. The traditional faith of the church plots a clear course for us to become partakers of the divine nature. Heretical speculations, which lead to licentiousness, are based on cleverly devised myths and result in destruction. Chapter 2 incorporates much of Jude's wrathful denunciation of false teachers and prophets. Peter like Jude sees variation from orthodox Christianity as involving moral deterioration. The heresy explicitly attributed to false teachers is skepticism regarding the second coming. This skepticism proves the nearness of the Lords return. We are urged to "be on your guard, so that you may not be carried away by the error of lawless men and fall from your secure position. But grow in the grace and knowledge of Our Lord and savior Jesus Christ."

I JOHN

The first epistle of John is filled with the same glorious revelation of Christ as the light and life of man as John's gospel. Though traditionally ascribed to the evangelist, scholars believe that the author of these Johannine epistles was an elder of the church in Asia Minor responsible for evangelism in the province. John's reason for writing is "that you may have fellowship with us and our fellowship is with the father and with his son Jesus Christ." This brief epistle tells us how to live the abundant and victorious life. Though we are born again of incorruptible seed and are new creations, we are prone to sin. If we refrain from hiding our errors, "he will forgive us our sins and purify us from all unrighteousness," (ch. 1:9). In verse 7 the Greek words used imply that through the shed blood of Jesus we are being continually cleansed and forgiven. Having the assurance that if we sin, we can be forgiven upon confession. We are told, "Whoever claims to live in him must walk as Jesus did." It is not God's will for us to keep on sinning but to have unbroken fellowship with him:

> Anyone born of God does not continue to sin; the one who was born of God keeps him safe, and the evil one cannot harm him. We know that we are children of God. . . . the Son of God has come and has given us understanding so that we may know

him who is true—even in his Son Jesus Christ. He
is the one true God and eternal life.

I John 5:18–20

In order to walk in the light we must love each other. Hatred and unforgiveness belong to the darkness and are incompatible with Christ, whose life is within us. This love is not an emotion, rather it is practical, manifesting itself in helping and doing good toward others. "If anyone has material possessions and sees his brother in need but has no pity on him, how can the love of God be in him? Dear children let us not love with words or tongue but with actions and in truth." Our every action is to be love motivated. Love of Christ and God must overflow into love of other believers (I Jn. 5:12). It is impossible to truly love God and not love our fellowman. Love is commanded (ch. 4:21). Faith in and love of Christ is the spur for us to obey him. His commandments are not burdensome legalities. Motivated by love we joyfully obey.

John warns us not to be led astray, "Test the spirits to see whether they are from God, because many false Prophets have gone out into the world." Any spirit or teacher that does not acknowledge Jesus Christ's coming in the flesh is not from God. The heresy of Docetistism, that Christ only seemed to become flesh and only seemed to suffer, is referred to as the spirit of anti-Christ. John states, "this is the confidence we have in approaching God: that if we ask anything according to his will, he hears us and if we know that he hears us—whatever we ask—we know that we have what we asked of him." Yet many of our prayers, seem to go unanswered. The key note is: "If we ask anything *according to his will.*" We are to be as closely identified with the Father as Jesus was. We are to live for him only, to continually seek his will, not our own. It is unthinkable that God would not answer Christ's prayers. If we attain that intimacy with him and "we are in him who is true—even in his son Jesus Christ," we will

205

see and experience the miracles of the apostolic age. We will also realize the glorious promise of a sin free life that John extends to us. John closes warning us to "keep yourselves from idols." Anything that comes between us and God's will for our lives is an idol and must be removed. Self-will, pride, sexual gratification, greed and pride are as abominable to God as Baal and Astaroath.

II JOHN

II John is addressed to a chosen lady (a church) and her children. The main commandment is "that we love one another. And this is love that we walk in obedience to his commands . . . his command is that you walk in love." A strick warning—even more sever than in I John—is given against deceivers (Docetists and Gnostics) who do not acknowledge Christ as coming in the flesh. We are warned not to afford such teachers the slightest welcome lest we share in their "wicked work." John expresses a longing to be reunited with the believers and hopes to talk with them face to face.

III JOHN

John is anxious to be released. So as in II John he expresses a reluctance to write and a desire to talk face to face. The letter is addressed to a dear friend, Gaius. Gaius is commended for his faithfulness and hospitality to John's messengers. He is encouraged to continue helping the travelling missionaries, and is warned about a false brother, Diotrephes. Diotrephes is a malicious gossip and is hindering the evangelists. John hopes to deal with him in person. Another brother, Demetrius, possibly the messenger delivering the three epistles is commended. The opening prayer, "I pray that you may prosper and be in health even as your soul prospers" shows that Gaius has his priorities in order! His spiritual growth is so obvious that the elder prays he may have as many material blessings as spiritual! This reflects Matthew 6:33, and we can be sure that no one who puts God first on a regular basis will go unrewarded.

JUDE

Traditionally Jude is ascribed to Jesus' half-brother, Joseph's son Jude. The author claims to be the brother of James the Just, Jesus' brother. The epistle was written especially for the churches is Asia Minor to encourage them to refute heresy. It warns very strongly against false teachers who "change the grace of our God into a license for immorality." Jude warns that these men "follow mere natural instincts and do not have the spirit." He condemns their greed, grumbling, immorality, and boastfulness. To Jude, sound theology was essential to sound morality. The heretic's (Docetist) sinfulness is a direct result of their deviation from the truth. Jude warns his readers to stand firm in the faith, to pray in the spirit, "stay always within the boundaries where God's love can reach and bless you" (verse 21, Living Bible). We are to love and comfort weaker brethren but hate sin. "Love the sinner, hate the sin." Jude closes ascribing honor to Jesus: "Who is able to keep you from falling and to present you flawless." We must continually look to Jesus and hold on to the true gospel, not allowing ourselves to be seduced by other doctrine.

REVELATION

Tradition holds that the Book of Revelation was written by the apostle John. However some scholars have argued that it was written from Asia Minor by a church elder, also named John, who was imprisoned on the isle of Patmos for preaching about Christ (Rev. 1:19). The Book of Revelation is a piece of apocalyptic writing. During the period from 170 B.C. to A.D. 70 this form of literature flourished. An apocalypse aimed to encourage the faithful to stand firm by reminding them that this present evil world system, which persecuted them, would soon be destroyed by God's personal intervention. An apocalypse expressed current events as well as teachings in images, symbolic colors, numbers, and creatures. To an outsider it would be meaningless, but the initiate could interpret. John wrote during the reign of Domitian to encourage the churches of Asia Minor and exhort them not to compromise with the imperial cult of emperor worship. A refusal to worship Domitian meant death. John aimed to make the rewards for loyalty to Christ so attractive and the punishment for worshipping "the beast" so fearful that his readers would gladly choose martyrdom rather than compromise. He made it plain that their was no middle ground. It was not possible to worship the beast publically and privately follow Christ. As the church faced a very real threat, we can be sure John intended them to fully understand the importance of his vision. The reason we find Revelation obscure is because we lack the "key" needed to interpret the symbols and figures used. The general meaning is clear as most of the images used are drawn from the Old Testament.

THE LAMB: JESUS
BABYLON: ROME
THE WOUNDED HEAD OF THE BEAST: NERO
THE BRIDE: THE CHURCH
THE DRAGON OR SERPENT: SATAN
THE BEASTS: EARTHLY POWERS
THE WOMAN AND HER CHILDREN: EVE/ISRAEL/THE CHURCH
666: NERO; POSSIBLY DOMITIAN/THE BALD NERO

As Revelation is a book of visions, dreams, and prophecies, like the parables of Christ its images speak to our subconscious, rather than conscious minds about spiritual realities.

Chapter 1 describes the vision John had of the risen Lord, "Alpha and Omega" the beginning and the end. He is the faithful martyr and witness, the example we must follow. Chapters 2 and 3 contain letters to the seven churches exhorting their members to be faithful even unto death. They are promised that through their death as martyrs they will be assured of a blessed and glorious immortality. Only one church is praised without qualification (Philadelphia), while the unfortunate Laodoceans are forever branded as "lukewarm—neither hot or cold. I am about to spit you out of my mouth." The lukewarm are condemned rather than those actively struggling with sin. Even the Ephesians though doing no wrong are told to "repent and return to your first love."

Chapters 4 through 21 contain a general message for the whole church. Chapter 4 glimpses the heavenly court and we are reminded of the awe and majesty of God. In chapter 5, Jesus, the lamb alone is found worthy to open the book of doom with its seven seals. The opening of the seals unleashes a series of judgements (disasters) upon the earth and its wicked inhabitants. The breaking of the first four seals unleashes the four horsemen: war, civil unrest, famine, and pestilence. The opening of the fifth seal provides a glimpse of the holy martyrs who cry out for justice. They are told to be patient for a little longer. This scene assures the persecuted churches that God will soon judge their tormentors and that the souls of the faithful dead go to Heaven, not to Hades. In chapter 7 the 144,000, the new Israel, are sealed. The number is symbolic; there is also a great multitude that no one can count present. In heaven they worship God day and night. They never hunger, thirst or experience sorrow again.

In chapter 8 a series of plagues are unleashed, but despite this the survivors are defiantly unrepentant. In chapter 11 the death and resurrection of the two witnesses occurs, and in chapter 12 the struggle between good and evil is brought out into the open, with Michael defeating Satan in the heavens and casting him down to earth. Many Christians believe we are living in the days described in verse 12: "Woe to you inhabitants of the earth for the devil hath come down among you having a great wrath knowing he has but a short time left." In chapter 13 the situation which occasioned the persecution of the Christians is brought out into the open. Two beasts appear. One symbolizes the emperors, dead and living, who are worshiped as divine. The other represents the imperial priesthood that enforced the imperial cult. The wounded head refers to the Nero Redivivus myth, the belief that Nero would rise to bring disaster to the empire. It is because the Christians refuse to worship the beast that they are being martyred. In chapter 14 the issue is clearly stated: "Fear God and give him glory because the hour of his judgement has come. Worship him who made the heavens, the earth, the sea and the springs of water,"(ch. 14:7). Rome will fall (ch. 14:8) and the worshippers of the beast will face God's wrath (verses 14–21). In chapter 15 the martyrs are seen in heaven rejoicing. In chapter 16 the seven bowls of God's wrath are poured on the earth. In chapter 17 Babylon/Rome is seen as a harlot, drunk with the blood of the holy martyrs, and chapter 18 contains the lament over her fall. In chapter 19, Christ on a white horse, with his army of martyrs destroys the two beasts and the kings of the earth. All the human followers of the beast are killed, and the beasts are thrown living into the lake of fire and brimstone. Satan is imprisoned in the Abyss for a thousand years, making possible the millennium or thousand year reign of Christ and the martyrs possible. At the close of the millennium Satan is released and gathers together the nations (Gog and Magog) who march against Jerusalem. They are consumed by fire from heaven. The devil is then thrown into the lake of fire (ch. 20:10). This is the climax of Revelation.

The second resurrection follows and the dead are judged. With all evil and the cause of evil removed, those who have been faithful to God are admitted to the New Jerusalem. Chapter 21 describes the beauty of the New Jerusalem in glowing poetry intended to evoke images of supreme splendor and all sufficiency. There is the river of life; the tree of life with healing in its leaves grows there. There is no more pain, sorrow, or death, and nothing impure can enter. "Now the dwelling of God is with men and he will live with them, He will wipe away every tear from their eyes. There will be no more death, or mourning, or crying or pain; for the old order of things has passed away," (ch. 21:3). The book closes with Jesus' promise, "Yes, I am coming soon."

Though we are not as familiar with the images used as the original readers, we can sense the vitality and urgency of the original message; we must keep the faith at all costs! In its time and place, Revelation enabled persecuted Christians to withstand the might and power of Rome. It gave them the vision and encouragement they needed to be overcomers.